Driving
on the

Wrong Side
of the Road

Driving
on the

Wrong Side
of the Road

*Humorous Views on
Love, Lust, & Lawn Care*

Diana Estill

Driving on the Wrong Side of the Road

For information, please contact:
Brown Books Publishing Group
16200 North Dallas Parkway, Suite 170
Dallas, Texas 75248
www.brownbooks.com
972-381-0009
A New Era in Publishing™

Paperback ISBN: 1-933285-41-9
LCCN 2006900552
1 2 3 4 5 6 7 8 9 10

www.dianaestill.com

Contents

Contents

Contents

Acknowledgments

SOME OF THE STORIES you're about to read have appeared in other print and online publications. I'd like to give special thanks to *The Dallas Morning News* for the initial chance to see my name in print and to *The Murphy Messenger* for providing space for my first weekly humor column. At a time when many considered the world too dangerous to warrant laughter, there remained those who encouraged me to keep writing humor. From my heart I wish to express to you my deepest appreciation. You know who you are.

To my husband Jim, the source of much of my entertainment and inspiration, the man whose love sustains my inner muse, how can I ever say enough? (He's no doubt wondering how he'll ever get me to shut up.)

Finally, I thank you, dear reader, for choosing this book when you could have selected one that promised to make you a millionaire or skinny within ten days. Now you and I can have a chuckle over those who fall for that hype.

Preface

COME JOIN ME ON a road trip, one that begins with a drive on Grand Cayman Island and ends with a detour through time. This adventure will take you deep into the cavernous corners of a treacherous mind and deposit you safely back at your original destination. Please remember to fasten your seat belt and hold on because otherwise you might get thrown into a serious state—and that's seldom a fun place to be.

The idea for this book grew from one of my humor columns first published in a local newspaper and later in *Road & Travel Magazine*. The story has since been circulated over the Internet, where it continues to amuse Americans who've either thought about or experienced driving a British car.

Our tour will take you through Texas, my home state, where you'll be introduced to the hazards of jalapeños, chain saws, and bad dogs. We'll explore the value of denim jeans, sharp knives, therapeutic massages, and digital cameras, too. I'll show you how to use carbonated mouthwash to turn your lawn lush green. And we'll discuss the theory of evolution by examining your refrigerator's contents.

Along the way we'll stop at a few historic markers (like "Prior wife: The final frontier") to review the significant past. But from there we'll move quickly to more present day challenges, such as self-checkout machines and gas-guzzling pickup trucks.

If you need a break at any time, you can put this book down and return to it later. It's not necessary that you see these points of interest in any particular order. So sit back, relax, and enjoy the views. Just remember that most of them will be totally skewed.

At the end of your trip, if you've enjoyed yourself or have a humorous personal experience you'd like to share then I'd love to hear about it. Please drop me a line at www.DianaEstill.com, where you'll always find my door open to welcome you.

Planes, Pains, & Automobiles

Driving on the Wrong Side of the Road

IN SEARCH OF ADVENTURE, I spent a week driving on the wrong side of the road. Well, truthfully, I was a passenger—but that only amplified my experience. You see, I'm the kind of gal whose vocal cords freeze in a crisis. My husband, on the other hand, is a screamer.

"We're going to be KILLED!" said he.

And since I had neither a steering wheel nor a brake pedal on my side of the car, I considered these might be his final words.

As usual, I'd reserved a rental car for our vacation. Only this time, we were on Grand Cayman Island—where locals drive on the left, and tourists sometimes forget.

We'd just left the airport in one of those Mr. Bean cars—essentially, a coffin with wheels. "Do you have the directions?" my husband shouted. He clenched the steering column, both hands fisted. "Do you know where the heck we're supposed to be going?"

Of course I did. I had the name of the town and our hotel address. And I had a rental agency map that looked like origami. What more did he want?

I spun the map several times until its printing righted. "We have to go north," I instructed, "toward Boddentown."

"Which way is *north?*" he demanded.

"What am I? A compass?"

"I'm about to crash this thing! Will you tell me which way to go?"

There was no need to yell. I was sitting close enough to feel his pulse, which was synchronized with the windshield wipers he'd inadvertently triggered. (The wiper switch was on the left side of the steering column where the signal lever should have been.)

He twisted and pulled at every knob within reach. "How do you turn these things off?" Swatting the signal arm, he set the indicators blinking in counter time with the wipers. All this added commotion caused him to brake hard and swerve left into a commercial driveway. Right then, one of the three suitcases we'd stacked in the back seat flew forward and clobbered him in the head.

By the time he'd regained his composure, the sun had set.

Traveling by twilight, we encountered the first of several "round-abouts," a vehicular intersection where cars circle at high speeds and nobody knows where they're going. We missed the bob-truck, veered into the right lane (which was the wrong one), and narrowly completed our connection.

From there we followed a two-lane road that had no streetlights, sidewalks, or shoulders. This left us competing for pavement alongside pedestrians, dogs, and overgrown bougainvillea.

"If we ever find this place," said my husband, "I'm parking this car, and we're staying put for the rest of the week."

I wanted to say something positive, but I couldn't. My intestines had a stranglehold on my esophagus.

After two passes, we found our destination hidden behind a row of flowering hedges. I looked at my mate and said, "I don't care if we have to live on our stash of airline pretzels and peanuts. I'm not getting back out there on that street."

But fear couldn't keep us in a death grip forever. Soon we realized we had to make a choice. Either persist or perish. So two days later, under threat of starvation, we ventured past our hotel lobby and out into the parking lot. "Other people do this," I said, peering out at Death Road. "We can, too!"

My husband nodded in agreement.

Just then, another Bean-mobile whipped into the hotel driveway and an ashen-faced couple spilled out from it. They stood gazing heavenward and making the sign of the cross.

I hoped they'd packed plenty of peanuts.

Shooting Whales
(With a Camera)

NEW TECHNOLOGIES SCARE ME, so I had to be shoved into the digital age. And like many, my first purchase was one of those new-fangled cameras. The ad for it said, "Everything you need to shoot, save, and share digital photos."

Euphoric at the thought of never again having to buy film, I selected one of those compact gizmos small enough to slip into my jeans pocket (baggy-fit, of course).

Soon afterward, I planned a vacation to Los Cabos, Mexico. And as luck would have it, my trip coincided with whale-watching season. I brought along with me both of my cameras—the new digital one and its film-dependent elder cousin—hoping to capture a picture that would entitle me to a lifetime of bragging rights. The more powerful zoom lens on my nearly-antique model could come in handy under certain conditions, I decided. It was entirely possible that giant marine mammals might possess a healthy fear of boats. And if so, whales could be reluctant to pose, close up, next to watercraft.

As it turned out, my assumptions were correct. Moby Dick wanted no part of a catamaran filled with seventy-five imbibing tourists. He leapt from the seas, glimpsed a fleet of sightseeing vessels in earnest pursuit, and then disappeared with a wave of a tail fin.

But soon the gray creature announced himself with a tremendous water spout. A rising half-moon of whale skin pierced through the cresting waves straight ahead. I fired my camera and waited to hear it confirm the shot.

Nothing.

Still nothing.

And then, finally, it went, "Zzzzz-ttt."

Checking the viewfinder screen, I discovered I'd captured an impeccable image of the horizon.

Undeterred, I readied myself for another round. I'd be more trigger-happy, next time. At the first sign of spray, I'd simply squeeze off an early shot and wait for the camera's delayed response.

"Oo-oo!" went the crowd in unison. I spun to my left and scanned the seas, searching for what everyone else had obviously witnessed. An enormous tail fin arced and disappeared, leaving me with a picture of a giant splash.

I hated this new camera. Somehow I resisted throwing the worthless piece of junk overboard. One of those ten dollar disposable jobs would have served me better.

Right then I remembered I had my old 35-mm wedged inside my fanny pack. Exchanging my digital failure for its film-hogging predecessor, I tried one more time. My finger twitched. My heart pounded. My knees trembled against the ocean's swells. And when the whale resurfaced, I clicked off three rounds in rapid succession.

Reassuringly, I patted my old friend, the camera I'd carried for more than a decade. Its case had been etched from saltwater and spilled sunscreens, and its date and time settings were no longer accurate. My antiquated companion was clunky, unstylish, and lacking memory. Yet it had once again tested reliable.

When it comes to providing everything I need, I think maybe cameras are a lot like spouses. My faithful 35-mm model flat beats out its younger, sleeker competition—because, frankly, what I need is something that'll snap on command.

Flight Facts No One Really Wants to Know

THE NEXT TIME YOU'RE on an airplane, if you want a laugh, read the safety procedures on that plastic card that's wedged in the seat pocket in front of you (and try not to think too long about why it's laminated).

Recently I flew on one of those vacation charters to Cancun, the kind where even accountants and engineers act like they want to "Par-tee ON, Man." If most of the passengers weren't drunk when they boarded the aircraft, they darn sure intended to be by the time the plane touched the next tarmac.

Being sober, and lacking the standard airline magazine I normally would have been reading, I searched for anything to help me forget that I was traveling aboard a flying tavern.

Earlier, a flight attendant had mumbled something over the P.A. system and then said, "Please take a moment to review the safety card in the seat pocket in front of you." I'd never before bothered to read one of these, as I'm not much on planning for catastrophes like airplane crashes.

I located the set of instructions that told me to follow the lighted exit signs in the event of an emergency. But I couldn't see the directional indicators for all the passengers who were right then clamoring in the aisles to find a lavatory. Ignoring the trail of antsy tourists with urgent bladders, I returned to my reading.

Passengers seated in the exit rows should be able to:

A. Open the door.
Does anyone know if he or she can really do this?

B. Maintain balance while opening the door.
Is there a sobriety test? Can these folks be served alcohol onboard?

C. Stabilize an escape slide.
Can these folks be served alcohol onboard?

D. Assess whether opening the emergency door will increase hazards to passengers.
Is there a minimum education requirement? Can these folks be served alcohol onboard?

E. Be at least fifteen years of age.
Do flight attendants ever card passengers?

My gaze shifted to the back of my tray table, to the words that read, "Fasten seat belt while seated." And I thought, *Well, how else could I do this? While standing on my head?*

In eighth-inch letters that I could barely make out, instructions for locating my life vest were written on the table's underside. Call me paranoid if you like, but I gained no comfort from learning that if the plane took a nosedive over the Gulf, I could clear my tray, secure its latch, fish for my reading glasses, and follow the step-by-step directions to help me locate, harness, and inflate a flotation device. However, I didn't dwell on this too long because I figured the life vest was hidden someplace I couldn't reach anyhow.

Unlucky in Luggage

IGNORING SUPERSTITIONS, I TRAVELED with my husband aboard a charter flight from Cancun to Dallas/Ft. Worth on a Friday the 13th. And though I crossed my fingers behind my back (and hoped NOT to die) during a couple bouts of air turbulence, once we'd landed I forgot all about any calendar associations with bad luck.

Standing at a luggage carousel inside DFW Airport, I checked my watch. At 11:00 p.m., the baggage claim area had emptied, and everyone else from our flight had moved on to Confiscations, I mean Customs.

Naturally, *our* suitcases had been lost.

"Those wet swimsuits I packed inside the dive bag are going to be pretty ripe when they get here," my husband said.

I'd forgotten we'd left Cancun with all our towels and beachwear still soaked. "They'll stink," I replied. "But as long as they're here by tomorrow, they'll be fine."

When our luggage hadn't shown up by Sunday, I turned to the tour operator for help. Right off, I inquired about the extra baggage insurance I'd purchased. And when their representative finally stopped laughing, she explained that, since our articles had been detoured on the homebound leg of our flight, I'd suffered no real inconvenience. Thus, I wasn't entitled to compensation for delayed baggage. (However, she offered that I might qualify for a reimbursement on my recent hair dryer replacement.)

"But what if my bags aren't ever found?" I pressed. "And what if, by the time they're located, everything inside them smells like a sewer?" Without any apparent sympathy, the agent told me that there were no precise guidelines for determining when luggage must be declared "officially" lost. And then she had the nerve to imply that most people are smart enough to know they shouldn't pack wet clothing inside a checked suitcase.

From there, the vacation packager turned me over to their insurance carrier, who directed me to contact the charter airline, my homeowner's insurance provider, and possibly Congress before submitting my claim. And after I reviewed their insurance documents, I discovered the policy contained an exception for items lost through "mysterious disappearance."

To stave off any more of my outbursts at their check-in counter, about a month later the charter airline graciously sent me a check for less than a third of my luggage contents' replacement value. The "During Travel Protection Insurance" (more like the "During OUTBOUND Travel Protection Insurance") I'd previously purchased, however, paid me nothing.

But this tale doesn't end there.

More than two months after their initial disappearance, our bags wandered back into DFW Airport. And judging from their smell, this likely triggered an evacuation inside Terminal B. The suitcases' reeking odors suggested our bags had been packed full of rotting fish, decaying potatoes, and about thirty pounds of wet potting soil.

No one at the airport would comment on (or for that matter, willingly touch) our luggage. So I tried to unravel the mystery of where these vagrants had been for the past two-and-a-half months. The bright yellow tags that read "Bundesgrenzschutz" were a dead giveaway. Obviously, our totes had been handled by illiterates.

Beneath the aforementioned garbled word I read, "Frankfurt, Germany." Best I can figure, somewhere along the way, the contents' mold had sprouted legs and decided to tour Europe.

Our expensive nylon dive duffle couldn't be salvaged. We took the odiferous bag as far as the garage before we opened its zippered compartments and stepped back. Instantly, hostile fumes escaped and seized me by my sinuses. "Yee-ow-ow!" I screeched. "We should have contacted a hazmat team!" Bleary-eyed and gasping, I felt inside the cavities for survivors. But only our fins and snorkel masks could be salvaged.

We buried my favorite swimwear, some towels, and a few shirts without a proper viewing.

Before shoving the dive bag into an outdoor trash bin, I studied the six-inch-long tag attached to its handle. The label that had been date stamped months earlier in Frankfurt read, "Expedite to DFW." All I can say is—maybe "DFW" is a German acronym for "distant foreign whereabouts."

Before Leaving Home

The Green Lawn Obsession

WHAT IS IT ABOUT a green lawn that'll make a man empty his wallet for fertilizer? Yes, I realize men ask the same question about women and shoes. But that's another matter.

Some think a home's exterior says a great deal about its occupants. Elaborate and well-maintained yards evidence successful owners. Or something like that. My landscaping theory, however, is less stringent. I think that every yard should have some greenery, and silk flowers and Astroturf don't count. It doesn't bother me if someone's lawn is a mixture of crabgrass, broadleaf weeds, and dandelions. When it's mowed, who can tell the difference between that and St. Augustine? Folks who see much better than I do. That's who.

But to my husband, a green yard ranks right up there with having spawned a child genius. Who cares if the toilet has been plugged for two days or the cat litter box threatens to trigger a neighborhood evacuation? By golly, our lawn looks lush!

Home improvement stores know there are plenty of men like him. That's why they carry 892 kinds of weed killers, 63 brands of pesticides—and only 2 types of plungers. The store clerks in these places, the ones who wear little orange aprons and typically run to escape me, take green grass seriously. You can't just waltz in there and ask for any old generic weed killer. Oh, no-o-o. First, you've got to identify what genus and species you want to eradicate. Then you must quantify the area of affliction and cite any specific challenges (such as a desire to retain existing trees or, in my case, an extreme allergy to yard work). Of course, you must follow the manufacturer's written directions when applying these chemicals—which then causes you to make additional purchases. And there you go, having to buy protective eyewear and rubber gloves and a month's supply of Cipro.

So I was thrilled when a caller to a local radio station provided an alternative. "You don't need any of these products to produce a green lawn," he said. Then he shared his crazy substitute formula—a concoction of cola, beer, liquid soap, mouthwash, and vinegar. I'm not kidding! The man said I only needed to mix these ingredients, spray the carbonated bathroom products onto my grass, and wait seven days.

Now some of you might scoff, but my husband tried this. And a week later, neighbors were asking if we'd suffered a water line break. Our grass was greener than pond algae.

This thrilled my mate so much that I decided someone ought to sell a premixed version of this instant-yard-of-the-month cocktail. Maybe it should be shelved in grocery stores on the same aisle with the bug spray and charcoal briquettes. And might I suggest stationing it next to the toilet plungers?

A Clean Fridge Can Raise Suspicions

A CLEAN REFRIGERATOR IS a sign of a bad cook. Mark my words, I know. I've seen many a spotless fridge sitting inside the kitchen of a flawed chef. You know the type I mean. They're the same ones whose floors would rival NASA's for cleanliness—women who not only mop frequently but hand scrub the grout lines. They clean fastidiously and refuse to fry anything for fear of splatter. No chicken-fried steak served there. No-sir-ee.

Now, if you open my refrigerator, the story is evident. You can find what we had for dinner last night, the night before, and probably the prior month because the leftovers are still in there, somewhere. They might be hiding behind an expired milk carton or lurking beyond a nearly empty two-liter bottle. But they're in there for sure.

I don't know why leftovers are so difficult to find once they're put away. But here's my theory: I think maybe food is always alive, even after we cook it. The process of heating and then refrigerating meats, vegetables, and fruits activates a cellular division of some sort. If you want a more scientific explanation, you'll have to go ask Stephen Hawking or maybe watch the Discovery Channel.

Anyway, once this process is set in motion, darkness (which occurs every time the refrigerator lights turn off) fuels it. So while you might think your Tupperware is safely preserving yesterday's culinary efforts, its contents are running the covert operation of sprouting legs.

During the night (or until you next open the fridge door), these containers crawl around inside your refrigerator. No one has ever actually photographed evidence of this. But how could they? The flash photography they'd have to use to capture this movement would halt any activity.

So, like I was saying, plastic containers and sandwich bags are afoot every time you shut them away. They move about, taking cover in door pockets, and hiding behind salad dressings, catsup bottles, and refrigerated pet medicines.

Whole fruits provide a different problem because they're completely unconfined. They roll themselves to the back of their clear, plastic bins where you cannot see them. Concealed, they smash themselves into mystery goo or disguise themselves as Chia Pets.

But cream cheeses are the worst culprits. They're the sneaky ones. They'll slide to the back of a shelf, wait at least a month past their expiration date, and then prominently move to the front again where your next houseguest will be the first to find and use them.

Lunch meats aren't a great deal better. I don't know what it is about sliced turkey that causes it to turn iridescent and shimmer like fresh trout. But I suspect there's some kind of reverse evolution taking place.

Oh, sure, you're probably thinking I should simply clean out my refrigerator more often.

To that I say, *What? Are you kidding? And have somebody think I'm a bad cook?*

A Sloth in Spring

PEOPLE WITH ALLERGIES ARE entitled to be lazy. I can say this with some authority because I'm one of these bleary-eyed, sneezing, wheezing, and gasping sufferers. A gentle breeze holds the power to incapacitate me for days, especially whenever the air is filled with pollens, dust, molds, and mushroom-forming fungi. This gives me an excuse to stay indoors and exempts me from seasonal labors for most all of March, April, and May . . . and a good part of September, October, and November.

It's not my fault that I can't weed my flower beds or rake the grass. I didn't ask Mother Nature to make me allergic to poison oak, hornets, wasps, and bees. All it takes is one sting or a brush with those "leaves of three" to turn me into The Alligator Woman.

While sitting safely indoors one Saturday afternoon, evading hazardous chores, I perused a magazine article about promoting good health. I couldn't believe it. The author practically accused me of being irresponsible.

First the writer had the gall to suggest I should walk every day for a minimum of thirty minutes. Then she said I ought to drink eight glasses of water daily, which I considered pretty redundant. If I consumed that much water, I'd spend more than a half hour per day running back and forth to the john. Next, the writer recommended that I avoid caffeine altogether and get plenty of sleep. Well, that further evidenced that this journalist didn't understand me. If I abstained from caffeine, I'd never wake up to begin with!

The article went on to say that I should limit the intake of antibiotics, and should assume more risks in life. I thought, *Ha, when your sinuses are as sensitive as mine, breathing is a risk.*

In disgust, I closed the magazine and contemplated joining my spouse in the backyard. Watching him made me feel guilty. He was out there crawling around on his hands and knees, pulling up broadleaf weeds and something I could have sworn was grass. It surely wasn't fair for me to be indoors, reading, while he labored in the heat with his shirt soaked in sweat.

I shut the periodical. But right when I did, a small card shot out and landed ominously in my lap. Maybe the paper projectile held some psychic message—possibly one intended to ward me from danger. Before I could read it, though, I choked up.

Fumes seeped upward, singeing their way into my nasal passages and burning through my throat. I stared at the perfume-soaked advertisement. Through watery eyes I could see that the scented paper contained the words "healing" and "garden."

Obviously, I'd purchased the wrong magazine because I'd intercepted a card intended for someone else—someone who doesn't have allergies. I tossed the hazardous note into the wastebasket. And then I decided it made sense to follow that advice about getting more sleep. So I took a long nap.

The Institute of Toiletology

SOME KNOWLEDGE SIMPLY ISN'T learned in traditional fields of education. It's gleaned from fits of frustration over home repairs and from the absence of a handyman when one is needed. In that sense, you might say that my house is the Institute of Toiletology.

"Which way does this go?" my husband asked one Saturday. He held an A/C filter in one hand and in the other, his reading glasses. Together we studied the cardboard square that looked reasonably the same on both sides. Spinning the filter several times, we searched its edges for clues. On one end, a line of arrows all pointed in the same direction.

"Okay, see," I said, indicating the arrows, "this side goes up."

"The unit doesn't have an *up*. It just has a part that faces toward the big square box and one that faces away from it."

"Well, then I guess the arrows point away from the unit," I huffed. *Gee whiz, how hard can this be?*

When the air conditioner quit working two years later, a repairman checked the great metal box in the attic (otherwise known as a condenser) and proclaimed he'd found the problem. "Right here's part of your trouble," he said. "Somebody put your filter in backwards."

So when I heard our master bathroom toilet trickling like one of those water therapy fountains, I knew right away we were in trouble. Lifting the top off the tank and studying the mechanical innards, I hoped to channel guidance from some wise plumber spirit, but I guess those experts were all out on other calls.

I didn't want to thrust my mitts into the tank, but then I remembered that it was a source of safe drinking water. I'd read that once, somewhere, though I'd seriously wonder about anyone who'd want to drink from the commode. I reached inside and lifted the black rubber sphere slumped against the water's surface. Instantly the toilet shut off. Problem solved, I thought to myself.

A while later, my spouse came home from work and announced, "There's something wrong with our toilet. It won't stop running."

I explained the fix, and then he, too, took the plunge—and once again the toilet silenced. This pattern continued for more than a week. Every time anyone flushed the toilet, its flotation device had to be manually reset. "Can't you fix this thing?" I pleaded.

"I'll work on it when I get back from my trip," my mate said. And with that, he departed on business.

For days I stared in stupidity at the lever attached to the bulbous nuisance. Possibly it just needed a new part, but I wasn't about to try to repair this myself.

When hubby came home and found the commode the same way he'd left it, he decided to tackle the toilet. From the kitchen, I called after him. "There's some kind of blue thingy on top," I said. "Something that's slotted like it's made for a screwdriver. Maybe it comes apart there."

"I'll check," said Mr. Handyman. And then a few moments later, he emerged, shaking his head.

"What? Did you fix it or break it?" I asked.

"No-o-o. I fixed it." He laughed. "All you had to do was adjust it by turning that blue thing a notch!"

Good grief. For two weeks I'd been waiting for *that?* I gave him an incredulous look.

"Wha-a-a-t?" he said. "How am I supposed to know these things? I'm not a toiletologist!"

Next weekend we're tackling a doorstop and a fence latch, and then we're moving right on to pressure washology.

The Media Room Conspiracy

HOME SALES TODAY ARE fueled by the appeal of three primary rooms: the kitchen, the master bedroom, and the media room. The first two of these make perfect sense because everyone has to eat and sleep. The last, however, confounds me.

I thoroughly understand the need for a roomy kitchen, one with plenty of natural light, ample cabinets, abundant counter space, and a walk-in pantry. However, at our house, we keep our camping equipment in the pantry and our 500-piece plasticware in the cupboards; we eat most of our meals out.

As for the master suite, it's always been a key selling feature. Nowadays it must be large enough to accommodate a king-size bed, and yet intimate enough for romance. Sitting areas are highly desirable, too. That's why many master bedrooms have a covey by the windows, one sizeable enough to display two chairs or, in our case, seventy-three paperback novels, forty-five women's magazines, several manuscripts in perpetual states of progress, and a houseplant that looks scarier than the one in *Little Shop of Horrors*.

Some master suites today are prewired for surround sound. Though, personally, I don't understand the need for more noise in the bedroom.

And that brings me to the final new-home promotional perk—the media room. I don't see what drives the demand for these expansive dark spaces. And I'll be the first to acknowledge that many don't grasp my need for a gourmet kitchen. So perhaps that makes us even.

I suspect media rooms are the result of a direct conspiracy launched by the consumer electronics industry. Yes, that's right. The electronics and stereo store directors probably got together with homebuilding industry officials. Together, they devised a joint marketing program they knew would stimulate high-priced television, stereo, and home sales. I bet their conversation went something like this.

Electronics Group: If only we could sell men *bigger* TVs—then we could make even greater profits. But you can barely fit a 54-inch screen into the average den.

Stereo Group: I know. And women really hate our new concept: woofer speakers that double for coffee tables.

Home Builder Group: Well, what if we built rooms sequestered away from the rest of the living space—vast empty areas where the sound can truly reverberate, rooms that cost next to nothing to add, rooms where the guys could put all their electronics and massively oversized TV screens?

Electronics and Stereo Groups: Oh, man! That would be great!

You see, these folks accurately suspect that the size of a man's television set is limited only by the space inside his home (as opposed to the one inside his head). Some women have even suggested there could be a "compensation complex" involved—a "my screen's bigger than your screen" mentality, if you will.

All I know is that I convinced my husband to buy me a better kitchen by agreeing to purchase a home that included a small media room. In the past two years, he's used that entertainment area six times. I won't bother to mention how frequently I've cooked in our kitchen.

But it's not only men who buy into the media room concept. Recently, a group of our neighbors stood outside discussing video electronic options. I caught my husband listening so intently that I thought someone might be divulging stock tips. Then I heard one woman say, "Oh, man, you should see the 100-inch screen we just put in! It's totally awesome."

My sweetheart's shoulders dropped. He smiled, attempting to hide his feelings. One hundred inches! I know that must have hurt. That's nearly twice the size of our screen, and it wouldn't even *fit* into our media room.

As you might guess, I'm already planning my next kitchen.

A Liar and a Leaf

NOTHING AGGRAVATES ME MORE than losing my high-speed Internet service when my cable connection croaks. This occurs about as frequently as Ashton Kutcher's mug appears in the entertainment news these days. And in my opinion, that's way too often.

My neighbors and I have formed a calling tree to report local cable problems. I mean, there's no sense in 150 people dialing the cable company to report an area-wide outage when 149 of us can dupe one person into ruining his or her day. This is not only fair, but it's the most prudent method to handle the situation. If we all had to argue with our cable service provider at once, let's face it, our community would no longer be a safe place to walk or drive.

Being especially talented at avoiding unpleasant tasks, I was one of the last to get roped into reporting cable problems. "Can you be home tomorrow between the hours of noon and four?" my neighbor asked.

"What does that have to do with me reporting an outage today?" I scoffed.

"You've OBVIOUSLY never called the cable company," she said, seemingly annoyed by this truth. She didn't bother to explain before

I agreed to dial Ontario or Mumbai or wherever the company's call center might actually reside. Cable companies are careful to locate their call centers outside our country. This discourages customers from driving over and physically acting out their frustrations. Otherwise, I'm certain that cable customer service employees would have to carry some kind of high-risk occupation insurance.

When I connected with a representative (whom, by the way, I could barely understand), our conversation went something like this:

Cable Rep: Hello. May I have the address you're reporting?

Me: Well, actually, it's an entire subdivision.

Cable Rep: I'm sorry, ma'am. I can only report a single location. Can you give me your address?

Me: Yes. (I supply my address.)

Cable Rep: I can have a service technician there to check out the problem tomorrow between the hours of noon and four. Will someone be at this address to let him inside?

Me: No. You don't understand. The problem is not *inside* my home. It's all over the entire subdivision.

Cable Rep: I don't have any way of knowing who else has a problem in your area, ma'am.

Me: But I'm telling you the problem isn't inside my home.

Cable Rep: Well, ma'am, it's sort of like this. There's a tree that has a problem somewhere—only we don't know where. So we have to start at the outer branches and trace it back until we find the broken location.

Me: Yes, yes. But you see, I'm not a branch. The subdivision is the branch. I'm just a leaf—or maybe a vein inside of a leaf.

Cable Rep: Exactly! You're a leaf. That's why we begin inside your house by checking your modem to make sure it's working.

Me: But I'm telling you that ALL of my neighbors are without cable service, too. So clearly it's not my modem!

Cable Rep: Ma'am. I know that's what you're TELLING me. But I have no way to PROVE that. So will you be home tomorrow between noon and four?

Me: No, I won't be.

Cable Rep: Would you like to reschedule for another day?

Me: No!

Cable Rep: Well, is there anything else I can do to help you, then?

Me: Yes! Get the big picture. And quit calling me a liar and a leaf!

Thank goodness it'll be someone else's turn next time. Because on my way to the grocery store that afternoon, I drove over a mailbox and six of those large, green rubber trash cans.

Samurai Kitchen

KNIVES ARE A PROBLEM in my household. Yes, knives. Not the Boy Scout kind or one of those lethal machetes, but the plain steak, paring, and butcher varieties. The issue is that my husband thinks the only good knife is one capable of slicing apples, shearing sheep, and trimming his beard. If the blade can't painlessly sever a finger, then who needs it?

I, on the other hand, think that knives should be tools of utility—not feared kitchen utensils. And since I can't shave my legs without requiring stitches, a sharp knife isn't something I care to have in my household.

"We *never* have a good knife in this house," my spouse frequently complains. Then he adds, "I'm going to buy you a set of *real* knives."

I take this the only way I know how—as a personal threat to my safety. "Go ahead," I say. "I won't use them. I don't want to get cut."

His typical response is, "That's what knives are supposed to do; they *cut.*"

As far as I'm concerned, he's the one who's being unreasonable. I'm only trying to reduce medical bills.

My samurai-wannabe spouse might have acquired this nagging

knife affliction sometime during childhood. Maybe he watched *Zorro* and envied his blade. Possibly he's seen one too many infomercials by Ronco. You know, the ones that suggest happiness is a result of turning cucumbers into . . . well . . . cucumber pieces.

What I'm trying to explain is that this obsession with sharp knives has altered the way we live, and it's become a source of embarrassment when shopping. I'll round an aisle, only to be confronted by the sight of my husband fondling a box of steak knives as if it's the Holy Grail. "Oh, look, Hon," he'll say, as I pretend he's talking to the woman behind me. "You *need* these," he'll persist, trotting after me.

"If you don't put those down, I'll be forced to use one of them on *you*," I say. Normally, this is enough to shake him off my trail. He'll return to the knife display, and then I'll make a beeline for the nearest checkout lane.

This scene has replayed itself so many times that I now cook only when he's not around to watch me do the food prep. Shopping has become a singular activity. And in conversations with my husband, I steer clear of using words that rhyme with "Henckels." Now if I could just figure out how to eliminate his exposure to Sunday morning infomercials, I could quit worrying about losing digits. I mean, without my index fingers, it would be extremely difficult to point and say, "I told you so."

How to Stretch 88¢

I DON'T KNOW WHY people spend so much money on cleaning agents. For eighty-eight cents, I can sanitize just about anything because that's what it costs to buy one-and-a-half quarts of chlorine bleach.

My relationship with bleach dates back to childhood when Mom treated my first wasp sting with a pinch of Purex. Instantly, the fire inside my forearm (where I'd just been stung) ceased. I guess you could say I've been a fan ever since.

What other product will do so much? Bleach will clean your toilets, wash your dishes, brighten your clothing, disinfect your kitchen, and quite possibly neutralize toxic waste. In fact, I bet the government could use it to eliminate Anthrax . . . which is why my terrorism survival kit contains fifteen rolls of duct tape, twenty gallons of purified water, a couple of flashlights, forty-eight batteries, one solar-powered radio, and three gallons of Clorox.

Anyway, I decided to combat a line of stubborn shower mold with a shot of straight bleach—because nothing else I'd tried had worked. Other tile cleaning products had sent me choking into a bleary-eyed attempt to contact Poison Control. (This reminds me that I should contact Heloise and tell her about my new money-saving idea. Forget paying $20 for mace. Instead, why not just carry a can of foaming scum remover?)

But let me return to my shower mold. Feeling confident, I retrieved an empty spray bottle from the laundry room and filled it with bleach. Then I patted the shower stall dry and attacked the blackened corner where a persistent fungus had defied death. I shot it good. "Take that!" I said, exiting the shower, spray mister in hand.

I stepped over the bath mat and crossed the floor to rinse the bottle in the bathroom sink. Then I dried the mister with a decorative hand towel sitting nearby. On my way back to the laundry room, I stopped to pet my cat. After I put away the spray bottle, I threw the guest towel in the washer with a load of laundry.

A little while later, I noticed my canvas sandals didn't match. One of them displayed a discolored patch the size of a quarter. No doubt, I thought, I'd dripped bleach onto the sandal. And right then it dawned on me. If I'd drizzled bleach onto my shoe, where else might I have spilled some?

Sure enough, besides my shoes, I'd ruined two bath mats, a good hand towel, and a couple other towels that had been inside the washer.

Feeling inept, I calculated the cost of my mishap: $29 for footwear, $40 for the bath mats, and $35 for the guest and bath towels—bringing the total to $104. This time, I conceded, it might have been cheaper to use tile cleaner. How could I have been so careless?

I called the cat over to me for comfort. On top of her head, she sported a conspicuous new white marking. Who would have guessed that eighty-eight cents could stretch this far?

Nocturnal Nuisance

IF YOUR HOME IS like mine, it's equipped with a number of alarms. And they're probably hardwired, supplied with battery backup power, and installed near your master bedroom. This lends credibility to the long-held theory that home builders are sadistic.

When an alarm sensor sounds at 2:00 a.m., my initial thought is to shoot first and check batteries later. But then I remember that's no way to preserve Sheetrock.

These safety gadgets malfunction so easily that I can set my smoke alarm off with my curling iron. And the carbon monoxide detectors, which share similar DNA with the common cockroach, are no better. They only activate during total darkness. Then, no matter what we do, we can't seem to kill their infernal, once-a-minute blare.

Recently, I heard one of those ominous beeps around 11:00 p.m. "Oh, no," I said to my already prone husband. "Either a trash truck is backing through our den, or worse, one of the detectors has a low battery."

In true take-charge fashion, my spouse pulled his pillow over his head.

"Well, aren't you going to do something?" I asked.

While Handyman hauled his ladder inside the house, I fished around in a junk drawer and found two loose batteries.

Beep!

"Which one was that?" I asked, staring up at the ceiling. "Was it the smoke alarm or that carbon monoxide thingy?"

Hubby scanned them both and said, "I can't tell. They're right next to each other."

"Which one is flashing?" I asked, irritated.

He peered down from the ladder. "Neither of 'em."

And just as he looked away, the carbon monoxide detector went *BEEP!*

I handed my sleepy spouse one of the batteries, and he shoved it into the needy little monster's mouth. We sat there for several seconds, anxiously listening. Maybe now we could get some rest. But about thirty seconds later, the alarm buzzed again. If I could have found the Energizer Bunny right then, I would have pounded him to death with his own drumsticks.

Trying the second battery, we achieved no better result. So we gave up and returned to bed—and one of us managed to sleep.

The next morning, my fully-rested husband departed for work, leaving me all alone with our screaming equipment. Mustering restraint, I drove to the nearest home improvement center instead of heeding the urge to burn all of his belongings.

I knew I'd have to sound intelligent if I wanted an employee to provide me with professional advice. So I asked the guy in electrical, "Do you think it could be that little square thingamajig?"

"You mean the 9-volt battery?" he said.

I nodded my head.

"Naw, I doubt it."

Bewildered, I looked at the man standing next to him—the one wearing an electric company T-shirt. The utility worker offered, "If you're not having a problem with any of the other alarms, that one's probably defective." He acted like he'd just let me in on some big trade secret. "If I were you, I'd just de-install it, and get a replacement," he said, straight-faced. "There's not but two wires in there. Just don't let them touch when you're pulling them apart."

When my husband came home from work, I pointed to the connections dangling from the hallway ceiling. "What did you do?" he asked enthusiastically. "Did you find someone to fix it?"

"Nope. I figured it out myself," I boasted. "But we've got to wait a few days for the new part to come in."

"How did you know what to do?" he pressed.

I shrugged.

Later that night, around midnight, the smoke alarm outside our bedroom went *BEEP!* And this time, I knew exactly what to do.

I'll repair the ceiling just as soon as the guy in Sheetrock tells me how to patch a bullet hole.

Disaster Preparedness: Approaches Differ

NEWS OF A PENDING category 4 hurricane causes me to imagine gas shortages, power failure, food spoilage, and possible tornados. However, my other half envisions a movie marathon, candlelight dinner, and potential romance.

"How are we holding up on chips and salsa?" my spouse asked as I inventoried our food supply. "Make sure we don't run out of chips."

"Did it occur to you that we'd need more than that to survive for days without power?" I replied.

"You're right," he acknowledged. "Do we have any chocolate?"

My husband is one of those wing-it-as-you-go guys, yet I'm a crisis planner. So as you might suspect, Hurricane Rita's approach caused plenty of stress at our house.

Before the storm, I asked if we had sufficient gas and emergency cash. Hubby offered, "I've got a half a tank and twenty bucks." Then he consulted the TV guide to see if the storm might interrupt the Dallas Cowboys' game.

"I hate to tell you this," I said, annoyed, "but you're not going to be watching that game if we lose power." He stared at me, wide-eyed at the thought of such deprivation.

The next day, I turned our home into what looked like command central for urban warfare. Flashlights, plastic tarps, and rolls of duct tape lined the kitchen countertops. Chargers engaged to energize cell phones and batteries. Several ice chests filed inside like soldiers ready for service, and a spare phone cord awaited deployment for dial-up access. I even went so far as to submit my next week's column—early!

"What are you thinking?" my husband beseeched. "It's a storm, not a nuclear holocaust."

"You'll be glad I did all of this when the time comes." I emptied our ice maker into a gallon freezer bag.

"What are you doing with that?" he asked.

"Making extra ice for the cooler."

"Well, I hope you thought to put some beer in it, too," he said.

The night before Rita slammed into the Texas/Louisiana coastline, Mr. Oblivious finally showed some concern. Local newscasts delivered stories of people stranded on highways without food, water, or gas. Statewide, major arteries were gridlocked. He stared at the TV set in disbelief, and then asked, "When are those library books due back?"

"*Library* books?" I echoed. "You're worried about library fines?"

"No, I'm worried about driving in blowing winds and bumper-to-bumper traffic tomorrow," he retorted.

I clicked my computer mouse and opened two more storm-related sites while the Weather Channel blared (for the umpteenth time) what sounded like an intergalactic battle theme.

The Fearless One lamented, "If I hear that music one more time,

I'm going to lose my mind."

It wasn't until the power failed and the tree limbs in our back-yard began snapping that my partner registered the magnitude of this event. "How can we be getting winds like this when we're two hundred miles away from the eye wall?" he remarked. But I didn't answer him. Right then I was trying to steady a flashlight over our homeowner's insurance policy.

"Did you know the bathtub in here is full of water?" my astute spouse asked from inside the bathroom.

"How else are we going to flush the toilet when the pumping station shuts down?"

"What? I didn't hear you." Circling the dim house, he called out, "Where the heck are you, anyway?"

"In here."

"Where?"

"Inside my closet," I yelled. "I heard a strange sound outside."

He stood in the doorway, laughing. "You're going to burn up in there with no air conditioning."

I smiled and pointed to the battery-powered spray mister hanging from my neck, a leftover souvenir from last year's Disney World vacation. "Not me," I said. "I plan ahead."

After the electricity was restored, we turned on the TV to get a report. But an electrical surge had fried our satellite receiver's innards. So we popped in a movie, curled up on the couch, and counted our blessings. You know, crazy as this sounds, sometimes I actually appreciate my husband's counter viewpoint.

Gender Benders

Football Terms for Dummies

DURING FOOTBALL SEASON, THRONGS of men thrive on nachos and "brewskis" and intentionally ignore their best interests—their wives. For football widows like me, this period can be frustrating. So I thought I'd offer a few sports definitions to encourage better marital communications. Both parties need to understand football terminology.

"Okay. The white lines mark yardage, but what's that yellow line?" I asked. I pretended to be engrossed in a televised football game.

My husband snapped, "It shows how far they have to go to make the first down." His tone revealed his irritation and the extent to which I'd interrupted his thoughts.

For a second, I considered his explanation. Surely the distance needed to make a first down changed with each play. Maybe he'd only half heard my question. After all, the TV camera operator *had* zoomed in on a bouncing set of mammary glands right about then. "Well, how do they get someone down onto the field to paint it so fast?" I pressed.

Anyway, if someone (I won't say who) had better communication skills, I might have understood that the yellow line was only a digital enhancement! It distorts the real image, kind of like those camera filters they use to video cheerleaders' thighs. (You'd never suspect those are the same gals who do the Dove ads, now would you?)

But I've digressed.

For those like me—people whose partners are incapable of breaking down football to its lowest form—let me define a few basics.

Football game—A game of physical challenge in which two groups outfit themselves to look like they've tripled their normal body bulk. Opposing team members, who hurl themselves at each other, pretend the fate of civilization hinges upon the control of an inflated piece of pigskin.

My team—Unless your partner has just returned from a corporate training event, "my team" refers to an imaginary assembly of football players who are either coached or quarterbacked by your mate. (Note: a precursor to "Fantasy Football")

We won—During football season "we" can mean "yes," sort of like it does in French. When your partner says, "We won!" you can pretty much interpret this to mean "yes" to anything you want for the rest of that day. (Important exception: "We lost" carries the opposite meaning of "yes." In fact, this phrase can suggest a number of performance issues for men—both on- and off-screen.)

Game day—The best day of the week to shop, especially when your spouse shouts, "We won!"

What? Are you blind?—A phrase yelled to no one in particular in an effort to displace latent authority issues. Typically, this habit is accompanied by a violation of some sort—most often to your eardrums.

Football pot—1. A seasonal expansion of girth or, 2. The elusive explanation for where your food budget monies have been disappearing.

Halftime—The sports-altered time frame in which all meals must be served even if this means sitting down for dinner at 4:00 p.m. Also the quantitative measurement used to compare the pace of meal consumption during football season to otherwise normal eating habits.

Fourth and one—A period of seconds preceding either an eruptive scream of jubilation or a dangerous time for house pets.

Hel-lo!—An expression that indicates your guy is sharing a virtual moment with the woman of his dreams. As in, he's pretending that if he could meet the half-nude cheerleader on the screen she might actually make eye contact with him. This presents the ideal time to mention that bald spot on the back of your fellow's head. Don't worry. He won't get mad . . . because you already lost him at "hello."

In some small way, I hope this has been helpful.

Spousal Arousal

UNLESS SOMETHING IS DONE immediately, our country's divorce rate is going to rise, along with its aging population. The reason for this can be summed up in one word: snoring. By the time we've reached middle age (according to unnamed studies cited by manufacturers of unproven snoring aids), 40 percent of us will sound like we're cutting our "Zs" with a chain saw. This stage-of-life symptom has given new meaning to the term "spousal arousal."

When he sleeps, my husband could be mistaken for a critically congested Darth Vader. At least that's how his snoring begins. But it moves rapidly to the teakettle stage, wherein he introduces a high-pitched whistle. This is followed by quivering lip actions more typically attributed to horses. And finally he adds some honking geese and a few snorting pigs to the cacophony. So now it sounds like Darth Vader has declared war on Green Acres.

My first thought is generally to try and stifle the offensive noise at its source. And then I remind myself that there are laws against this.

One night, I was determined to block out the audio emissions from my sleeping Star Wars wannabe. From a nearby drawer I retrieved a pair of ear warmers, the kind that clamp flat to the head. The double layer of polar fleece might serve more than one function, I decided. And, sure enough, minutes after I'd fitted the headgear in place, I fell fast asleep.

About an hour later, I awoke, after first dreaming I was being strangled by a snake, to the rumble of a full barnyard. Bolting upright, I panicked when I couldn't see anything out of my right eye. And then I realized I was being blinded (and choked) by a set of ear warmers.

The next day, exhausted, I turned to authoritative sources for help. Right off, I found techniques to combat snoring in W. Bruce Cameron's book, *How to Remodel a Man.* One of his recommendations caught my attention. To paraphrase, Cameron suggests that the non-snoring partner should pretend to be asleep, and every time the afflicted party snores, the other party should awaken him with a blood-curdling scream. I rather liked the concept, but I felt it required too much energy. And as it turns out, there are medical procedures available to help overcome this relationship-destroying habit (snoring, that is, not screaming).

Snoring, for the most part, is caused by vibrations of the tongue, nasal passages, and soft palate. Research has proven that by searing a sufferer's throat with a special laser, reducing their tongue size surgically, or shrinking their uvula (that hangy-down thing in the back of the throat), this health hazard can be improved. In fact, merely mentioning these remedies to your loved one ought to do the trick. But you must remember to periodically reintroduce the topic. Otherwise, your bedmate will forget and begin snoring again.

Last night, my husband suffered one of those memory lapses. He snored so loud I feared he'd trigger the neighbor's car alarm. As I lay there, trying in vain to pretend he was a giant purring cat (possibly a feline version of Clifford), I remembered the scream technique. Maybe a sharp elbow to the ribs would work equally well, I considered. It was worth a try.

Each time my hubby snorted, whistled, or honked, I lovingly gave him a quick jab, and when I did, his breathing immediately returned to normal. (I wasn't getting any sleep, but the entertainment value alone made this worth doing.)

A few dozen pokes later, the whole activity struck me as amusing. I credit this lapse in judgment to prolonged periods of sleep deprivation. Anyway, I snickered and tried to stifle it but found I couldn't. With my hands clamped over my mouth, I was determined to not laugh out loud. Nonetheless, within seconds I'd succumbed to the giggles and fully rousted The Villain of Darkness. He rolled over and found me cackling in a fit of hysteria.

"What's the matter with you?" he demanded.

I couldn't answer him because my tickle box refused any mercy.

"You've got to stop thinking about your humor column," he barked. "For Pete's sake, will you shut up so I can get some sleep?"

This, as you might expect, made me roar.

Why Men Grill

IN CASE YOU'VE NOTICED your man (or someone else's) behaving strangely these past few weeks, let me explain what's happening. It's outdoor grilling time. My advice to any woman witnessing this phenomenon is to simply relax and let the guy have his way. Otherwise, you'll end up back in the kitchen.

I know. You're going to complain that the meat is undercooked, smells like Lea & Perrins (which, I might add, contains anchovies), and tastes like scorched underbrush. And when you attempt to check on the broiling progress, you can't find the cooker for all the smoke and flames. Well, all I can offer is that I've learned to eat around the edges of my hamburger, and I've taped the fire department's phone number to my patio door.

Ladies, it's not ours to question this primal ritual that connects men to their earliest caveman counterparts. Let's face it. Bonfires and fresh kill have a greater history than, say, Viking and Albertson's. This explains why a guy who'll regard the kitchen stove top as though it's something that might give him estrogen has no problem tackling a backyard barbecue. First, he's genetically encoded to build fires. And second, his reptilian brain tells him that, at least to cavewomen, the scent of crackling meat over an open flame is an aphrodisiac.

In the Paleolithic Period, there were no dating services or Internet. A caveman had to depend on the size of his smoke spirals and the waft of sizzling meats to lure a prospective partner. Or to put this more directly, the bigger his blaze the better were his chances of finding "wooka-wooka" that night. So don't misinterpret your fellow's intentions. He's not trying to burn you out of your home. He's just saying, "Hey, Baby, I'm ready for wooka-wooka!"

In earlier times, cavewomen probably had a choice of fireside dinners to attend. Before making a selection, they no doubt scanned the horizon instead of the personal ads. Our female ancestors reasoned that large smoke plumes indicated a sizeable roast (or else another cheap blind date trick). Hence, the guy with the biggest column generally won the girl.

Whole industries have been launched around man's inclination to continue this kind of competition. Consequently, retailers now bring us barbeque pits so colossal they require trailer chassis, and smokers capable of cooking an entire herd.

When it comes to charbroiling, it seems everyone has climbed onto the chuckwagon. Any day now I fear I'll be unable to enter Home Depot due to the grill display that's consumed the remainder of the parking lot. (Though my absence might make a lot of summer workers happy, it would be horrible for shareholders.)

My husband is one of these barbecue warriors—but he competes only by degrees. His infrared Texas Incinerator-Master (guys will buy anything that includes the word "master") reaches 1,600 Fahrenheit and will sear a filet mignon in two minutes. It also can, I've discovered, melt plastic forks from four feet away and eliminate entire sets of wedding Tupperware.

I do my best to stay away from our backyard beast (the grill, not my spouse). That's my man's territory, and I don't want to infringe. Some sort of alchemy is happening there. A combination of brawn and blaze is transmuting into . . . well . . . wooka-wooka. I figure if I can't take the heat, I should stay in the kitchen.

Massage: A Touchy Subject

AT FIRST I TRIED to hide my illness, but eventually I had to confess. I suffer from a chronic massage phobia.

Unfortunately, I forgot to share this information with my daughter until it was too late. She'd already purchased gift certificates to treat her father and me to a full body massage. And I didn't have the heart to tell her that I'd only redeem mine if I could remain fully clothed—in a scuba wetsuit.

If I had a figure like one of those actresses on *Desperate Housewives*, I might feel different. But my curves bring to mind women like Kathy Bates instead of Teri Hatcher. I'm overwhelmed by the thought of exposing my naked imperfections (and dimples on the wrong end) to anyone other than my spouse. Furthermore, I don't want another man to squeeze on me unless he's a doctor, paramedic, or Richard Gere.

My body has the consistency of a waterbed; push it here, and it bubbles up over there. Why would I want an innocent stranger to suffer the task of kneading my bloated belly? I already receive those services from my cat.

Neither my husband nor my daughter sympathized. Both insisted I use my gift coupon before it expired. "I'll be right there with you," my spouse encouraged. "It's no big deal. You'll love it. I promise."

Reluctantly, I agreed to go.

Right off, I knew I was in trouble when the spa attendant said, "You'll find your robe and *spa panties* in the dressing room."

I sought my partner's reassurance, but someone already had escorted him away. What in the name of Vanity Fair was a spa panty?

I easily found the designated terry cloth robe, though nothing inside the dressing area remotely resembled underwear. I decided to ask another victim, I mean patron, for help.

"Oh, they're right over there," the lady said. She pointed to a box on the countertop, one just large enough to hold a few dozen shoe "footies." I thought maybe I'd misunderstood. But then I reached into the container and pulled free a strip of gauze paper connected on two ends by a half-inch elastic band. And let me assure you, one size could NOT have fit all.

I waddled out, wearing my robe and adjusting my paper g-string, only to encounter the spa director standing next to Mr. Universe. "Fabio (not his real name) will show you to your room," said the attendant.

A surge of terror, or maybe it was hormones, shot through me. I sputtered and stammered, and when I'd finally recovered asked, "Could I please have someone else? Preferably a female?"

The attendant gave me a knowing look, as if instead of revealing modesty I'd just divulged my sexual preference. And then she called to a twenty something-year-old worker whose jeans stopped four inches short of her navel. The statuesque, model-thin masseuse had thighs no bigger than my wrists. I did my best to appear pleased.

"Is this your first massage?" asked Amazon Girl. (I've no idea how she could tell.)

"Yes," I responded. Then quickly I spouted, "My daughter bought gift certificates for me and my *husband.*"

Inside a dimly-lit room, the trendy blonde smoothed her hands up and down my spine. As she pressed her oily palms into my congealed fat, I prayed she wasn't psychic enough to divine my thoughts through touch. Otherwise, she'd know I regretted my decision to enjoy a high-fiber breakfast that morning. Telepathically, I willed her not to rock anything that could produce gaseous emissions. In that coat closet-sized room, there was no way we'd both survive.

When my session finally ended, I rejoined my husband. "They tried to pair me up with a man!" I cried, indignant.

"So? They gave me a woman," he retorted.

"What! Did you send her back and get a man?"

"Are you kidding?" he said. "If I had, there's no telling *what* they might have thought."

Would you believe Massage Phobia is contagious? My husband now has it, too.

Wedding Anniversary Gift Guide

WEDDING ANNIVERSARIES REMIND US how far we've traveled with our spouse. For better (as is my case) or worse, we've survived some period of shared history together. So it's important to commemorate these mile markers by giving our mates appropriate gifts. Some of my personal recommendations include jumper cables, reading glasses, and wireless headphones. Or you could skip the jumper cables altogether and spring for an AAA membership.

Racking my brain this year for gift ideas, I checked that dated wedding anniversary guide created in the late 1800s by blacksmiths and dry goods store owners. Okay, other than me, no one actually credits them for devising this gift list. But come on. Who else would have chosen copper, steel, iron, tin, silk, lace, leather, and cotton as anniversary presents? They cleverly moved all the good stuff (silver, pearl, ruby, sapphire, gold, and diamond) to the end—past the twenty-fifth anniversary mark—which wasn't fair. Back then, men rarely lived long enough to reach these obligations.

Looking over this anniversary guide, I couldn't help thinking how much it needed another revision—one that might make the suggestions more practical for current times. For instance, the old guide recommends that the first anniversary gift should be made of paper. During earlier times, most couples simply exchanged letters and cards on their first wedding anniversary. But today, breathing strips (those plastic bandages you stretch over your nose to keep nasal passages open) are a better choice because nothing promotes marital harmony like a good night's sleep.

The third anniversary is an ideal time to purchase those wireless headphones. Really. Most of them have leather earpieces so they even agree with the traditional guide. You and your spouse will never again argue over your television volume. As an added benefit, whichever one of you is wearing the headphones will now have a legitimate excuse for having not heard the baby cry, a plea for help, the phone ring, the doorbell sound, or the dog barf.

By the time you get to your fifth anniversary (and so few do anymore), the traditional list suggests a gift of wood. I think it's bad taste to encourage baseball bats for anniversary gifts. Duct tape is much more suitable.

Let's talk about that tenth year, which is the tin/aluminum anniversary. Could we dispense with the case of beer? That's just plain tired. The tenth anniversary ought to warrant a more extravagant present, like maybe a cruise for one.

I checked the guide to see what type item I should give my spouse this year, and it said ivory. Obviously, the traditional route won't work. I'll have to resort to something more suitable, which is why I thought of technology. Oh, sure, I've been coveting my neighbor's laptop computer. But you don't think that has anything to do with my choice, do you?

No. I wouldn't dream of purchasing a computer for my spouse so

I could use it during the day while he's at work. That would be just as self-serving as the Christmas he bought me a set of stainless cookware (to encourage me to prepare more meals at home). Or the time he gave me a sewing machine (to save money on curtains). Or the year I received skimpy lingerie, just so . . .

I wonder which he'd prefer: a standard or extra-wide computer screen?

The Filing Fairy

IT'S BEEN SAID THAT sex, money, and children are the top three subjects married people fight about. If so, then the fourth must be tax preparation.

Yes, the IRS is directly responsible for family discord at tax time each year. I'm sure of this because only during tax season does my spouse notice my filing habits. And now that state sales tax has again become a permitted deduction, my spending habits have come under microscopic scrutiny, too. Where, I ask you, will this end?

Part of my problem, I'll admit, stems from childish beliefs. You see, I hold faith in the Filing Fairy. How else can I explain the news clips in my credenza, the bills in my buffet, and the bank statements in my laundry room? I can give no other reason for the kitchen countertops I last saw in 2002 (when we moved in).

Go ahead. Laugh if you like. But if you think about it, it's not a great stretch to believe in fairies. No greater than, say, believing you might retire comfortably on social security—or that there's such a thing as fair taxes, honest political campaigns, or diets that'll work for anyone.

Now, I'll admit my theory has its drawbacks, especially when I need to find something incidental like a birth certificate or a deed-of-trust or my passport. And my marriage suffers because my husband doesn't fully grasp this situation. Fairies are elusive beings tethered to no timetable, a concept that's difficult for me to explain to him at tax time.

"Do you have the receipt for the printer we bought last year?" my mate asked. "You *did* file that receipt, didn't you?"

"Of course I did," I said. "I've got every receipt . . . for the whole year." I jaunted into the guest room closet and retrieved a shiny gift bag. Displaying the package as though it might be a new purse, I added, "They're all right *here.*"

"Right *where?*" he asked, staring at the sparkly sack dangling from my wrist.

"Right here!" I turned the bag upside down. What followed resembled a Wall Street ticker tape parade. A rain of sales receipts, deposit slips, and ticket stubs fluttered like confetti to the floor. I won't bother to mention who provided the cleanup, but I will say this experience proved educational. I now know that it's possible to fit 3,742 receipts into a small gift bag, and that I can't count on the Filing Fairy to keep a schedule.

Still, I believe—because I can't afford not to.

So if you see the Filing Fairy in your area, please let her know that she's overdue at my place. And while you are at it, pass along that same message to the Laundry Leprechaun, the Ironing Imp, the Garage Genie (the one who organizes, not the one who opens the garage door), and the Gardening Gnome. When they all show up, I'll be in sheer marital bliss.

Prior Wife: The Final Victory

THERE'S NOTHING FUN ABOUT beginning a new marriage with mementos from your spouse's prior one. My philosophy is this: it's difficult to create a "present" using other people's pasts. So my husband and I bought all new furniture when we blended households.

We agreed we were going to start fresh. Thus, rarely did I miss the chance to ask the critical question, "Where did this come from?"

Most of my husband's belongings had origins I found acceptable, and those that didn't held some sentimental value I could understand; that is, all but his cactus.

Now, how can anyone make a big deal out of a houseplant, you might ask. Well, first, it was four feet tall and artificial. Second, this Saguaro replica was a decorator's nightmare left over from an earlier failed marriage.

But don't get me wrong. I don't mind bad taste. It's just that if I'm going to display any of it, I want it to be my *own*.

When my partner decided to keep this plastic, prickly protrusion, I tried to be reasonable. I really did. Perhaps it held some intrinsic value I couldn't see, though to me it seemed nothing more than a green, vertical monument to history—something to be eradicated and not preserved.

Over time, this imposter became a fixture in our den. Its terra-cotta, concrete-filled base etched deeply into the carpet. I could have sworn it was trying to take root.

For five years I glared at that cactus, wondering what magic the monolith possessed. On several occasions I suggested its obsolescence. But whenever I did, my fellow would just pause, look at it, and say, "*I* still like it."

Our two cats were enamored with it, too. They used the cactus limbs for a scratching post (and sometimes as a tree-climbing simulator). Eventually, the felines managed to snap off one of the monster's long tentacles.

At last, the nuisance was damaged beyond repair! Fighting the urge to pick up the broken limb and wield it like a Jedi light saber, I pronounced it dead at the scene. Hubby reluctantly agreed.

Imagine my elation when the familiar CURBSIDE PICK-UP, THIS WEEK ONLY sign appeared at the end of our block. My mournful mate hauled his longtime companion to the sidewalk, placing the broken cactus arm by its side. Observing this, I considered how I might best express my sentiments.

Maybe I should go out and whack it a few times with its own appendage. You know, just to be sure I've fully purged.

The next morning, my husband arose early and peered out our front living room window. Did he think fairies had come in the night to revive that thing? I couldn't help but laugh at him.

"Yes!" he exclaimed, turning to give me a celebrated look.

"What?"

"Someone took it last night! I just knew *somebody* would want it," he said.

When I relayed this story to a close friend, she offered, "Why, sure. I put out an old table, and it was gone in less than an hour."

To whomever took that cactus I'd just like to say this: if I were you, I'd watch that thing closely. It has serious staying power. But I've proven once and for all that I've got more. And that victory, I have to admit, was sweeter for the wait.

Routine Maintenance

Food Addicts Seldom Fight Fair

HAVE YOU EVER NOTICED how, generally speaking, one food addict will tend to marry another? Then if one partner changes any dietary habits, the other resorts to sabotage.

My husband and I both have food issues, though I'm the only one who'll admit this. When I suggest to my spouse that he might have an eating disorder (as in, to him "all you can eat" signals a challenge), he scoffs. "I don't have food issues," he'll say. "I *love* food." Consequently, his blood has the same sugar level as a trainload of Twinkies.

Sometimes, my fellow overeater will make himself a second slice of toast (slathered with peanut butter), and then he'll cut his eyes at me and ask, "Do you want half of this?"

It's sweet of him to check, and I'm grateful he's thought of me. But I usually give him an appreciative look and say, "No, thanks."

"Good!" he'll exclaim.

Unlike most wives, I don't split meals with my spouse. Nuh-uh. I've learned better. When I tried sharing fajitas with him once, he thought my half should be the onions, peppers, and rice. And when I agreed to split a seafood platter, he gave me the baked potato and shrimp tails. If meal sharing ever becomes a part of my weight management plan, I'll probably die of malnutrition.

But now the worst has happened. My food lover received a dictate from his doctor. Cholesterol-lowering medications aside, he's been ordered to change his diet. So I agreed to help by removing from our home several forbidden foods.

While sitting at our kitchen table discussing ways to improve household temptations, I caught my husband's hand. He'd been nonchalantly clawing into a sandwich bag full of oatmeal cookies. Mindlessly, he prattled and chewed at the same time.

"What are you *doing?*" I shrieked.

He stopped, and stared at me for a second, and then, deadpan, replied, "Well, I thought they were going to rot."

We were not off to a good start. I snatched what was left of the cookies and opened the trash bin.

"No! Don't do that," he begged. "I'll have to fish them out."

That was several weeks ago, and now I'm going through withdrawal myself. My partner's diet has caused me to become a hoarder of all things fried, processed, or sweet. I've begun hiding contraband in the one place I know he won't look—inside the pantry, right next to the spare paper towels.

Oh, you're probably thinking the pantry is a place he frequently visits. And actually, that's true. In fact, he wanders through there more often now that he's been told he can't have goodies. However, the poor dear suffers from an acute genetic affliction that affects only males—something called PB (Pantry Blindness).

As long as I wedge my sweet rolls, cookies, and potato chips between the spices, canisters, and household cleaning supplies, the Cookie Man can't see what he most craves. Even when he stares straight at these items, all he observes is a mass of unidentifiable shapes and colors. It's a debilitating disorder, one I've often cursed but now find somewhat advantageous.

Despite my cleverness and deception, I've had to give up a few basic food groups altogether. For instance, ice cream. Instead of Blue Bell for dessert, I'm now substituting yogurt with yeast cultures the size of Cleveland. And in place of red meats, I'm relegated to gnawing on raw vegetables, salads, and dried floral arrangements. Honestly, I don't know how much longer I can take this.

So if my husband claims he can't find me, please don't worry. I'm probably here, standing inside my pantry—right next to the paper towels.

Diet-friendly Party Food

WITH THE ONSET OF fair weather comes the return of social activities that can easily become food orgies. Family reunions, block parties, and outdoor cookouts provide the perfect settings in which to test your dietary limits or, in my case, intestinal fortitude. I try to restrict myself to two servings—of each item. You might say that I've never met a casserole I didn't want to wholly consume.

But these days, it seems that most everyone adheres to some kind of diet, whether it be the low-carb, sugar-busting, reduced-fat, South Beach, or North Pole (nothing but sushi) variety. One diet guru insulted me by suggesting that only French women naturally know how to maintain optimal weight. Well, all I can say is that I've visited a French restaurant, and there's no mystery involved; the French are stingy with their portion sizes. Good grief. What's next? A book entitled *The Prison Diet* by Martha Stewart?

This national obsession with weight loss causes me to cry every time I'm invited to a party. Generally, I'm expected to bring a dish, one with something inside it. But it's just too difficult to figure out what I can cook that everyone will eat. Thankfully, my last invitation was straightforward.

It said, "Bring sandwiches."

Sandwiches are simple. Two slices of bread with something, anything, wedged in between. What a relief. All I needed could be found in one trip to the grocer.

Inside the supermarket, I stood in the bread aisle, contemplatively studying an assortment of packaged loaves. The 9-grain version would impress the health conscious. But if 9-grain was good, maybe 11-grain was better. No, wait. Was it whole grain or whole wheat that contained the most fiber?

The sugar-free, whole wheat, low-carb loaf clearly won out over the oat bread I suspected better reduced cholesterol. But then I spotted the raisin bread, which tastes wonderful with pineapple cream cheese. Dieters on Atkins could have the cream cheese with the low-carb bread, but not the raisins, I recalled. Maybe I'd fix tuna salad instead.

Moving on to the canned meats, I remembered the mercury issues that plague tuna fish and opted for chunk chicken. Now, all I needed was some mayonnaise, celery, and apples for my chicken salad. So I grabbed the fruit and a few stalks of celery and then wheeled my cart to the condiments section. There I encountered thirty-six kinds of salad dressings and a matrix of comparisons I could no longer make without consulting the FDA. Overwhelmed, I put back the chicken, the apples, and the bread, and traded the celery for a fresh, leafy head of Romaine.

"What's this?" asked several partygoers that night. I was shocked. In today's diet-prone culture, how could anyone not recognize low-fat mozzarella lettuce wraps?

Beats the Chi out of Me

I'D NEVER BEFORE HEARD of Chi, other than when I'd visited a few overpriced coffee houses. Wasn't that some kind of spiced tea? The party invitation I'd received suggested Chi was somehow related to fitness therapy. Whatever it was, it sounded metaphysical and hip—so I decided to check it out. Possibly my Chi was out of whack, and I didn't even know it.

As it turns out, according to the Chi representative, my body is filled with toxins. Considering the paint thinner I drank and those plastic curtains I ingested when I was a child, I had no difficulty believing this. To make matters worse, the fitness saleslady said my blood might not be getting enough oxygen. Judging from the difficulty I was having with memory recall, I considered this, too, merited attention. Otherwise, one day I might be found wandering the streets, lost, in search of curtains sold only in the Dollar General store!

The party hostess told me not to worry. Her Chi machine would be my cure. First, she asked me to drink a sixteen-ounce bottle of water and to lie down on the floor. Suddenly, I recalled what it was like to undergo a sonogram. Already, I could feel those toxins pressing my bladder and insisting upon release. And the Chi machine hadn't yet been turned on.

Lying prone, I placed my ankles in what resembled a foot massager (or maybe prison stocks). According to the woman who talked nonstop, this toaster-size apparatus would oscillate at the precise speed required to render maximum therapeutic benefit. She flipped the switch, and away I went flopping like a hooked bass. My thighs darted in one direction while my hips dashed in another. My head danced as if it were attached to my body by a coiled spring. Not since I'd overslept for school and awoke to find my mother shaking me by my feet had I experienced such a sensation.

After three minutes on the Chi machine, the rep advised, I would feel the evidence of what had transpired (besides me looking like an idiot). Something called the "Chi rush" would flood through me as soon as the gadget was switched off. And sure enough, I tingled from toe to crown when the relentless device stopped. This must have been caused by the oxygen rushing to my brain so it could yell at me, "Suck-er-er!"

"Cancer can't grow in oxygenated blood," the Chi lady explained. I nodded as if I'd just finished studying this in med school. I thought to myself, *So all I need to do is vibrate for several minutes a day to prevent cancer?* And then I made a mental note to check and see if jackhammer operators are listed last among cancer-prone professions.

Next, the Chi expert instructed me to lie still while she placed a half cylinder-shaped object over my midsection. Again, I remembered prior medical procedures—specifically my MRI experience. At least my head was free, and I wouldn't feel like I'd been buried with a pulse this time. This gadget, the woman said, was called a "Hot House," and it emitted FIR ("far infrared rays"). Pondering her words, I couldn't help but wonder if I might exit looking like a Chernobyl victim.

"Radiation?" I yelped. "Is this harmful?"

In her best Chi voice, the saleswoman assured me I was in no danger. She said the low-level infrared rays from the Hot House generated less radiation than my own body.

Well, I thought, if I'm already producing it, how bad can it be?

A purple light like the one inside my manicurist's nail dryer flickered on. The Chi woman carefully pointed out that the Hot House contained some sort of crystals. I wondered if they were Australian, Waterford, or maybe Swarovski.

But here's the *amazing* part. This gizmo supposedly burns more than nine hundred calories per hour and will improve everything from constipation to diabetes. I'm not kidding. Some of the sales literature I found on various Internet sites suggested it could even enhance my bust size.

A warm feeling penetrated my torso, the kind you might experience if you were, say maybe, shoved into an Easy-Bake Oven. But I felt no discomfort whatsoever. If I can lose nine hundred calories in an hour like this, sign me up!

When my session was over, I asked, "How much do these things cost?" That must have been the question the saleslady was waiting for because she appeared almost tongue-tied from excitement. In fact, she couldn't exactly tell me the prices, so she handed me a sliver of paper. The quote sheet listed four-figure amounts that exceeded my mortgage payment.

Someone more astute might have expected that these Chi machines are sold only through multi-level sales. I should have been suspicious—if not of the product, at least of anyone who repeatedly utters superlatives like "great" and "amazing."

"Do you think there could be something to this whole Chi thing?" I asked my husband. He'd not shared my Chi experience, but he expressed his usual skepticism.

"If the products were all they're billed to be, then why wouldn't they be sold in every Wal-Mart, Target, and Best Buy in the country?" he quipped.

I'd asked this same question of the Chi professional, and she'd offered, "Maybe they don't know about it." I echoed her comment.

"Well, sure. That makes sense," my partner said with a tone. "Maybe this technology is so top secret that Brookstone and Radio Shack haven't yet discovered it." I had to agree. That didn't seem plausible for products that are made right here in the United States, especially given that they're sold by at least three multi-level salespersons in my hometown (population 8,000).

But I didn't want to form hasty conclusions. Like sugar pills, these machines might really work for people who believe in them. I dozed off to sleep, confident that for now I was fully oxygenated and cancer resistant.

The next day, just as a test, I stood in front of a clock and shook my hands violently back and forth, timing myself for two minutes. Though this process proved tiring, I simply had to know. Sure enough, my suspicions were confirmed. The moment I quit flapping my fingers like they were covered with fire ants, I felt that familiar "Chi rush." And later, when I checked, would you believe my bust size hadn't changed one bit?

Hope in a Box

HE STOOD THERE WISTFULLY staring at Suzanne Sommers, Denise Austin, and Kathy Ireland, while I tried not to notice. "Did you know Suzanne Sommers has always remained between a size four and six?" my husband asked.

It'll take more than *that* to intimidate me. "Didn't she marry a cosmetic surgeon?" I asked, refusing to look at him.

I mean, really, it isn't fair that actors and models profit by packaging hope in boxes of workout equipment. It leaves the rest of us thinking that, with only a few dollars and a vivid imagination, we might look as good as these promotional photos.

I continued strolling about the store looking at ski simulators and stationary bikes. Briefly, I wondered why I'd subjected myself to this humiliation, and then I remembered that vacation photo of me sliding on a giant plastic saucer down a sand dune. The cameraman (yep, it was hubby) had chosen an unflattering angle: top of sand dune, rear side of wife. That picture, I humbly noted, didn't look a thing like the one on the cardboard box I'd just seen.

Humph! If he wants to see a body like Suzanne Sommers's, then he'll have to stand in the sporting goods aisle more often.

So why do we fall for this? Everyone knows these envied women didn't get their sculpted bodies from twenty minutes of butt busting three times a week. No-sir-ee. It requires thousands of dollars of liposuction, tummy tucks, and fanny lifts to overcome the effects of sagging. I mean, aging.

Yet, in spite of this, I can't help believing that maybe . . . just maybe . . . I could look like that if I really worked at it. Cosmetic surgery, on the other hand, is out of my realm—both financially and emotionally. I can't imagine going under a knife for any reason that could be considered "elective."

Well, I don't think that remaining a size six (yeah, I used to be one) holds any likelihood for me. At my age, I'd be happy to improve body tone and maybe drop ten pounds. So for now, I'm going to try this silly push-pull-extend-retract thingy my husband talked me into purchasing.

Yes, I succumbed. All it took was one look at that well-oiled Adonis displayed on the box. "Oh, look, Honey," I said. "Let's get *this* one!"

The Summer Size Cycle

BY AUGUST, MOST PEOPLE I know are looking forward to the fall season. They've had it with the heat, drought, and arrhythmia-provoking utility bills and are ready for milder temperatures and round-the-clock televised football. Anxiously, they anticipate weekends that won't include weeding, trimming, and lawn mowing. And when you think about it, these activities are silly anyhow. Here you are, running your sprinklers until your water bill spirals to triple digits for the sake of your yard, and all you're doing is causing the grass to grow faster, which forces you to mow it more frequently and leads you to shower more often. It's a vicious cycle.

Anyway, since I don't earn enough to pay my electric bill, and I'm not the one who maintains our lawn, I cling to the final days of summer as if they were my life raft. And to some extent, they are, because the rest of my calendar months unfold like this:

September

Celebrate two birthdays, one anniversary, and the start of football season with cake, brownies, and ice cream galore. Heat swimming pool to extend its usage. Sneer at neighbor's autumn door wreath.

October

Purchase Halloween candy two weeks in advance. Honor Daylight Savings Time until husband reports he's arriving at work early enough to see the cleaning crew. Put away ivory-colored shoes. Taste Halloween candies to make sure they're good. Check bathroom scales to see if they need recalibrating.

November

Bake banana nut and pumpkin breads three weeks before the holiday and store them in the freezer. (Save a couple to snack on before Thanksgiving.) Preserve leftover Halloween candy bars in gallon-size plastic bags. Store oranges and grapefruits in the garage to increase refrigerator space for holiday dishes. Consume previously purchased fundraiser fudge to make way for homemade recipes. Hide bathroom scales.

December

Attend six and host two holiday parties wherein all the social interaction occurs around a table full of cookies, pies, and cakes. Purchase four types of coffee, six brands of cereal, two dozen eggs, a pound of bacon, and a box of pastries to accommodate family members staying at the Estill B&B. Stack boxes and gift-wrap materials someplace where they won't be in the way . . . like maybe on the treadmill.

January

Take down the Christmas tree and pack up the decorations. Throw away rotted fruit accidentally left inside the garage. Resolve to lose ten pounds by the end of the month. Polish off the last of the pastries my guests didn't eat. Serve nachos made from leftover holiday cheeses on Super

Bowl Game Day. Break out the bathroom scales and recalibrate them (by setting the dial to negative five). Consider fasting until, say maybe, Lent.

February

Encourage spouse NOT to buy chocolates for Valentine's Day. Eat the truffles anyway after he disregards this request. Rearrange closet so that stretch-fit and elastic-waist pants are now at the front, and short, tight skirts are hidden in the back. Glare at bathroom scales.

March

Buy Easter eggs for the grandchildren. Throw away (or eat) any remaining Halloween candy to make room for the leftover marshmallow bunnies. Search new spring catalogs for swimsuit styles with knee-length skirts.

April

Remove holiday boxes from treadmill and run for five minutes (less if winded). Purge house of all remaining sweets. Place 9–1–1 call to Jenny Craig.

May

Congratulate self for losing five pounds. (I did remember to reset the scales, didn't I?) Celebrate weight loss by making homemade ice cream on Memorial Day. Steadily increase workout intensity and duration because autumn will be here before you know it.

Much like watering and mowing the lawn, it's a self-defeating cycle.

Harnessing the Horsepower

The Gift Horse

IT'S NOT UNUSUAL FOR a child to want a horse. But in my case, I not only desired to have one of these ton-and-a-half beasts, I wanted to be one. I'd play with my cousin Jana, and tell her, "Let's pretend we're horses, and *I'll* be the white stallion." She probably wanted more to play with Barbie dolls, but being two years younger, she obliged me.

Overhearing our conversation, my grandmother would stop us short as we galloped through her kitchen. "Wouldn't you rather be a mare? Don't you know stallions are boy horses?" she'd ask, emphasizing gender.

All I knew was that stallions were the ones in the spotlights when I watched *Fury, My Friend Flicka, The Lone Ranger,* and later, *Mr. Ed.* Nobody except Grandma, who, alongside Grandpa, cattle farmed in Frisco, Texas, ever mentioned mares.

By the time I'd grown old enough to know the difference between a filly and a colt, I'd decided life wasn't worth living without one of these worshipped creatures. But I then lived in the suburbs. And Dad insisted there were ordinances against parking ponies in our garage, a fact that failed to faze me.

During the daytime I read *Horse & Rider* and *Western Horseman* magazines, studying up on curry combs, bridles, hackamores, and tips on hoof polish. The way I had it figured, manifestation was nine-tenths preparation. I didn't know how I'd get a steed or where I'd put one when he arrived, but one was coming soon. I just knew it. My parents wouldn't want me to die at the tender age of twelve. They'd take note of my absence from the dinner table, see my ever-fading complexion, witness my permanent hundred-yard stare. On this I'd bet everything I owned, including my entire collection of plastic horses—even the Palomino.

Mom and Dad expected my infatuation would pass, and I'd soon move on to the next developmental stage, one where I'd be searching for something they better understood and for which they thought horses were a mere substitution.

"I'll take you to the riding stables," Mom said, hoping to return color to my jowls. "How's that?"

This wasn't exactly the response I'd been hoping for, but I considered it a partial concession.

Saturday afternoons at Green Acres Riding Stable actually made the whole situation worse. Every week I rode Big Boy, a tall, muscular, Palomino gelding I hoped to eventually own. Mesmerized by his flaxen straw mane, his enormous chocolate eyes, his soft prickly muzzle, I sketched his image during classes, envisioned how he'd look with his tail braided, planned what color ribbons I'd use for our first parade. My unwashed jeans safeguarded the musty sweet after scent of our vigorous rides together, ones we shared despite the stable hand's warnings. "Don't give 'em his head. Be careful. Make him walk." I'd nod, compliant, and then as soon as Big Boy and I were out of sight, I'd gig him and pretend he was a unicorn.

By the time Christmas rolled around that year, Grandpa decided my craving for all things equine had endurance. So he bought me a white Welsh pony named Cotton (who coincidentally was a mare). He said I could keep her in his cow pasture and ride her anytime.

I stood there, looking at Cotton's short, frail legs. Mentally, I compared her to Big Boy, a quarterhorse with a gait as smooth as meringue pie. And right then I regretted ever having galloped through Grandma's kitchen.

A Crop of Knowledge

FROM FIRST THROUGH SIXTH grade, I had the luxury of attending the same school, growing up with the same friends, and traversing every footpath between my home and the corner grocer. But the summer I graduated from elementary school, my parents stunned me with an announcement. We were moving from suburbia to the country.

Already, I was going through puberty and suffering from an acute fear of junior high school. Now, they'd added another dimension to my pain. I'd have to adjust to remote living, fewer shopping options, and worst of all—a telephone party line. No teenager should be subjected to such suffering, I felt sure. At thirteen, my social life had ended even before it had really begun.

Our new house was located off a white rock road drizzled with oil, about three-quarter miles from the nearest patch of pavement. Five of its ten accompanying acres were cultivated. The remaining five had been left as pasture, land for which I had a planned use.

In that kind of "you-owe-me" attitude teens are apt to display, I felt that, if I had to live on a farm, my parents should at least buy me a horse. Dad, of course, thought differently. He always did.

My father was the kind of guy to whom you didn't dare suggest you were bored. In fact, he'd rattle off a list of chores longer than the Mississippi if he heard any of us kids mention boredom. Quite often, he assigned us tasks to ensure we didn't have time to grow unenthused. Prison labor. That's what my brothers and I called it.

While performing these exercises in humility, I often carried on an internal dialogue that went something like this. *Maybe if I sing or hum, this won't seem quite so bad. Mm-hmm-hmm-mm. I hate him, I hate him, I hate him.*

Crouched to the ground, my back turned toward the afternoon sun, I hummed while I pulled weeds. Sometimes a leafy culprit would break free at its roots, and I'd cringe. Dad would notice the botched job, for certain, because he held "inspections" every evening when he arrived home from work, and if I hadn't achieved his idea of perfection, there'd be more chores to do tomorrow. I buried the exposed roots with a little topsoil.

One sizzling morning while I was working in the fields, it occurred to me that a person should do a good job, not just because he or she was fearful, but because it made him or her feel good to do so. I stopped thinking about what a tyrant Dad was for taking me away from my friends and for making me labor like an indentured servant. Instead, I experienced the rich, moist, black earth between my fingers, and the pink, wriggling worms beneath the soil. I turned my face toward the sun to catch its renewing energy. And when in the distance I saw a flurry of white dust, I ran into it and reveled in the heart of the whirlwind. I had not observed these things before, though they had always been there.

That first summer in the country taught me the significance of solitude. Bobwhites whistled in the mornings and cicadas whirred in the afternoons, replacing the more familiar sounds of automobiles and children at play. I no longer cared about the telephone party line. These new sounds provided my connections to the world. However, I still pined for a horse.

The following spring, I decided it was time to assert my desire for live transportation. "Dad, I *have* to have a horse," I said. "If I don't get one, I'll just die! Nobody who lives in the country does without one. Nobody but me."

Dad registered no emotion. After a lengthy pause, he finally spoke. "Tell you what I'll do," he said, folding into his chair at the dinner table. "I'll plant that three acres out there in ok-ree." He pointed with his knife toward the kitchen's south window. "It'll be producin' by summer."

Now, I might have been a city girl, but even I knew that horses didn't eat okra. I waited to hear where this was going.

"All the ok-ree you pick this summer'll be yours," he continued. "You can get your momma to drive you to the market to sell it."

I glanced at Mom. She gave no protest.

"You'll make enough money by the end of the season to buy you a horse," said Dad. And with that, he went back to eating his dinner and offered nothing more.

Wait. I don't know anything about okra. How much will three acres even produce? Will it be enough to really buy a horse? How fast will it grow? How often will I have to pick it?

This was going to be another one of Dad's tricks like that move to the country. Another one of his many attempts to teach me something of "value." But what choice did I really have? If I wanted ever to get a horse, I'd have to play along.

Every morning when the school bus pulled away from our house, I surveyed those three acres. Hundreds of thick, hairy stalks jutted from the ground. As the school year drew to a close, I thought less about acquiring a horse and more about what kind of deal I'd made with Dad.

Well, I'll just rotate my schedule, I told myself. I'll pick only one acre a day. Then every third day, I'll begin again where I started. That'll make this project more manageable.

But some additional research on okra yielded unwanted news. I learned that okra plants can produce two or three pods per day, pods that must be picked while they're small enough and sufficiently soft to eat. If a crop is overlooked for a few days, a full week's produce can be lost.

Darn him! He's done it to me again. He's found a way to make me work through my entire summer vacation!

I was furious by the time I confronted my trickster. "Dad, I'll have to pick okra every day to get enough money to buy a horse."

"Yeah. I 'spect so," he said, matter-of-factly. He gave me a wry grin.

My first harvest took more than two hours to complete. By the time I arrived at the market that afternoon, I was saturated with sweat and breaking out all over in a rosy rash. An old farmer wearing coveralls took my bucket of green. After dumping the contents onto a produce scale, he proclaimed its value. "Eggs-act-ly sixty-six cents, Young Lady," the old man chuckled.

For a moment I considered this guy and my dad might somehow be related.

Sixty-six cents? Is he serious? I worked a whole two hours for sixty-six cents?

I'd been suckered again.

With my meager earnings, I purchased a pair of much-needed plastic gloves.

Later that evening, I whined to Dad. "I did just what you told me to do. And do you know how much money I made?"

"No." He scooped a few peas across his plate and into his mashed potatoes. "How much?"

"Sixty-six cents!"

"Well, it'll get better. Crop's just come in." He took a long drink of his iced tea, swirling the cubes as he set down his glass. "Just give it a few more weeks."

My younger brother snickered.

Mom gave him a scolding look.

"Yeah, well, I'll probably have to work even *harder* then," I huffed.

"Ye-ah. You prob-ab-ly w-i-l-l," he said, savoring every syllable. Then I witnessed that smirk on his face. I hated it whenever he smiled at me that way.

Within a couple weeks, sure enough, the stalks grew five feet high. They appeared to walk themselves closer together every night. Due to the blazing summer heat, I rose each day at six-thirty a.m. and began plucking pods by seven o'clock. Later, I'd find myself coated in a fine layer of okra hair that I'd transferred from my plastic gloves to an array of body parts. I might just as well have rolled from head to toe in poison oak.

Cold showers and sheer determination carried me through that summer. And by early August, I'd earned $75, enough money to purchase Stardust, an eight-year-old Morgan gelding. Stardust became my trophy and my transportation. I felt proud to have worked and earned the funds to buy this steed all by myself.

It's the details that often escape my memory. Maybe some things are more easily recalled than others. However, I vividly remember that the first time I rode Stardust, I shot Dad a smirk.

A Deck of a Time

THE SMELL OF MOLDING leaves can only mean one thing: it's time to launch an outdoor project. One fall, I searched diligently for cheap skilled labor to build an outdoor deck, and I wound up begging the only available carpenter I could find—my father.

By asking Dad to help me, I'd essentially agreed to relive puberty, only in a slightly taller body. And just like old times, I caught myself acting like a fourteen-year-old, alternating between respect one minute and defiance the next.

For insight, I'll share that I've always suspected Dad views women as God's factory seconds. Or more directly, he equates Y chromosomes to superior brain power.

On command, I passed him the electric drill, tugging the cord to give it some slack.

As the oldest of four children, I'd previously participated in count-less outdoor projects with Dad. Translated, this means I'd been given ample opportunities to pour concrete, shingle roofs, mend fences, lay tile, spread gravel, stack lumber, pound nails, and render aid as a human tool caddy.

Dad pointed with the drill. "Pass me that square."

Square? What square? I don't see a square. What did he do with it? Oh, wait. Is this it, underneath this board? This thing that looks more like a half-square?

He handed me the drill with one hand as I pressed the L-shaped object into his opposite palm.

I grasped the cold, heavy, boring instrument, eyeing it carefully. The plank beneath my toes awaited screw holes, but a drill was something I'd never been permitted to operate. Decades earlier, Dad had taught me not to mess around with power tools. And here I was, a grown woman, still following his orders.

"String that saw over here," Dad said. That's Dad-speak for, "Bring me the skill saw."

Dutifully, I complied.

A red carpenter's pencil leapt from Dad's midriff and fell to the ground, yet he ignored the tool's escape and kept sawing.

The air around me wafted with the aromas of Old Spice, damp leaves, and fresh sawdust—creating sort of an autumn potpourri. I scurried to retrieve the pencil and handed it to Dad before he'd even missed it. Without glancing up, he stuffed the runaway back into his shirt pocket and continued working.

In my left hand, I gripped the drill and squeezed its ominous black trigger engaging it once. Z-z-z-z-ing.

Hmm. That didn't vibrate as much as I'd thought it would.

Z-z-z-z-ing. Z-z-z-z-ing.

Laying the next plank into place, Dad surveyed its fit. Silence. (That meant it met with his approval.) He lifted and inspected the two-by-six. "This one'll have to go this side down," he said. "Got a knot in it."

I nodded as if right then I'd been thinking that same thing instead of critically evaluating his discount store boots.

Forever the carpenter's helper; never the carpenter.

What would it feel like to actually wield the power of a drill, skill saw, or maybe even a welder? My brothers had known these experiences. And it seemed to me that they'd been admitted into a special fraternity. (But since they'd never thrown any good parties, I didn't care.)

Maybe I'll drill just this one teeny-weeny hole while he isn't looking. Z-z-z-z-ring-ing-ing.

And a perfect hole it was. I examined the new cavity I'd created from countless years of mental practice.

Dad stopped working, blinked hard a couple of times, and stared at me for a moment. (Probably he was checking to see if I'd accidentally hit an artery.) Then he returned to marking a notch he needed to cut and pretended like nothing extraordinary had just happened.

I sank a screw into place and drove it home, wondering when I'd find the nerve to say, "String that skill saw over here when you're through with it, would ya?"

On the Backstretch

Turning Fifty with Oprah

WHEN I TURNED FIFTY, I wanted to know more about the year of my birth. What else had happened back then? What had women my mother's age been experiencing around the time I entered the world? Before I could evaluate my life's progress, I needed to find out.

Both my mother and Oprah's delivered a daughter in 1954, which means I passed the half-century mark the same year as did "The Queen of Talk Show." That realization caused me to note my comparative lack of success. Oprah owns her own television studio and magazine—and I own my own computer.

I'm also as old as another well-known star (which is not to suggest that these two icons are in any way related). So, in theory, I suppose I should take stock. While I'm not as wealthy or famous as Oprah, I've managed to age somewhat better than Godzilla. At least the last time I checked, I had fewer scales.

I don't know why so many people resist the idea of turning fifty. Personally, I'm enjoying lower auto insurance premiums, AARP membership benefits, the Reader's Digest Big Print Edition, and restaurants' senior discounts.

Oh, sure, there are downsides to this stage of life. But they're nothing that can't be managed by plastic surgeons, personal trainers, and a daily glass of orange juice fortified with particleboard.

Seriously, having a fiftieth birthday is an honor, an accomplishment in and of itself. It's a sign of good health and stamina, or, in my case, proof of chaos theory in action.

When I turned fifty, so did M & M peanut candies, TV dinners, and the Tasmanian Devil. So you can see, I was in pretty good company. While researching my birth date, I discovered that in 1954 some visionary developed the first shopping mall. At last, I'd found an explanation for my addiction to Bath & Body Works and tile flooring. The phrase "born to shop" would henceforth carry new meaning.

The same year I was born, fish sticks debuted in the US, RCA pioneered the color television, and a woman in Alabama earned the distinction of being the first human ever struck by a meteorite while sleeping. Well, maybe there were others. But if so, they didn't live to document their bad luck. (You probably think I'm making this up, but I'm not.) The victim was inside her house sleeping on her sofa when an eight-pound rock crashed through her ceiling and slammed into her thighs. Imagine this: one day, interstellar debris could smack someone seated on a toilet!

Nothing truly eventful happened on the *exact* day of my birth, unless you count running the world's first FORTRAN computer program as anything besides geeky. I found this information particularly troubling because the only college class I ever failed was a programming course in FORTRAN. Nonetheless, I'm now vindicated because I outlived this obsolete language. Most likely, I survived longer due to the fact my decisions don't follow a flowchart (and that makes me a whole lot easier to comprehend).

I can't help wondering if I'll live long enough to become a centenarian. Who can predict? I mean, all I have to do is avoid the mercury in fish, limit my exposure to television, sunlight, and crowds—and remain alert for inbound meteors. For someone born in the year of the fish stick TV dinner, the ones advertised on color televisions sold inside malls and viewed best from living room sofas, it seems I'll have to rely on luck.

Time for a New "Do"

WITH SUMMER LOOMING AND my Christmas weight still firmly attached to my hips, I decided there was no time like the present for change. Yep, I needed a new hairstyle.

Truthfully, the idea came to me a few weeks earlier when my husband and I had been sitting inside a performance hall filled with, how shall I say this, mostly mature patrons. We were among the few midlife attendees present. Everyone else appeared well beyond retirement age.

At intermission, my astute spouse whispered to me, "Have you ever noticed how all women past a certain age have the same basic hairstyle?"

He was right. I scanned the audience, deftly noting the number of shaped necklines and exposed ears. Some had longer layers than others, but overall these ladies shared the same coif. And ever so humbly I realized . . . mine was a direct match!

This couldn't continue, I told myself. So I immediately did what any woman does when she's searching for a new "do," one she can call her own. I made an attempt to find out what younger gals were wearing.

Perusing through three hairstyle magazines, ones I hoped contained cuts that might flatter a face like mine, I made an astonishing discovery. They do not hire people who look like me, or women who have manes like mine, to become hair models.

I kept flipping the pages, thinking, *Come on. Just find someone with short, thick, wavy hair, preferably someone with a slightly asymmetrical face, and see what kind of hairstyle worked for them.* But this proved both futile and humiliating. I might as well have picked up *Vogue* while I was at it and searched for a dress that would look flattering on a 5' 3" overweight fifty-year-old.

Why had I made such a pointless purchase? What had I been thinking? My answers were not going to be found inside these rags. No way could any hairdresser make me look like Jennifer Aniston or even Sharon Stone. And I would never resemble a soap star or a twenty-something-year-old model.

I guess most everybody is trying to look like someone else. Yet deep down, women don't really want to resemble each other at all. We simply want what we perceive someone else has obtained—like maybe Brad Pitt, or famous thighs, or perpetual youth. And so we search for ways to emulate those who have what we're seeking. We copy each other's makeup tips, manners of dress, and yes, hairstyles, hoping to find the magic key that'll provide access to our elusive goals.

By the time most of us have reached a certain point, we've recognized the insanity in this—the foolishness in our fawning over appearances. Now we just want easy maintenance, something that'll let us "blow and go." Who's got time for curling (or flattening), picking, gelling, scrunching, and shaping? Leave that for the girls. We mature ladies are much too busy for such time-consuming efforts. We've got club meetings, dinner parties, and performances to attend. We've got books to write, gardens to plant, and travel adventures to plan. So it's easy to see why we might all adopt the same no-nonsense hairdo. It's not that we don't want to appear unique or hip. It's just that we've all arrived at the same conclusion: it's only hair.

A few days after I'd bought the magazines, I tried to explain to my stylist the look I desired. She gave me a sympathetic smile and said, "I know exactly what you mean. You don't want that typical old-lady hairstyle. Neckline shaved, ears out."

I couldn't believe it. Whom could I trust? My husband had noticed, and my hairdresser had known better, and yet for five years, they'd let me walk around looking my age.

Empty Nests

HE TOOK ONE LAST look over his shoulder at the television and the assemblage of used furniture and industrial-strength trash bags that bulged with clothing. Everything he owned fit into the back of his pickup truck. From his stance, he appeared ready to roll out from under my rule and into the dominion of dormitory existence. I felt my heart rise into my esophagus.

Come on, now, I said in my most cheerful manner of self-talk. *This is the day you've been waiting for. No more dirty laundry in the living room floor, size ten shoes left in the kitchen, and snack-cake wrappers found under the sofa. You won't ever again need to search underneath his bed for missing cups, bowls, and silverware!*

"Well, it looks like this is it," my little-boy-turned-football-jock said with a grin. His green eyes glimmered in the morning sun. Obviously, *he* was happy. Why, then, was I feeling all weepy and mournful?

He staggered toward me in a playful fashion, his arms outstretched to hug me goodbye. It was one of those full-body embraces—the kind where neither of you wants to let go. I could barely get my chin over the top of his shoulder. Why hadn't I recognized before how much he'd grown? The answer came quickly; I hadn't hugged him that way in years.

Maybe he hates me now. Maybe I didn't give him all the things he needed during his childhood, and now this *is* it! Maybe he will never come home to visit. I'll just receive a belated Christmas card each year, one with two or three sentences scrawled inside.

Tears pooled underneath my chin. What about all those family vacations we kept putting off? There were so many places I'd wanted to take him, but there were football games that couldn't be missed and girlfriends with whom he'd already made plans for the weekend. Where did the time go?

I watched as he drove into the sunrise of a new day—a day unlike either of us would ever again experience. Well . . . almost.

He was back and forth so many times that first year of college that I lost count of the number of weekends I saw him. The sight of his pickup truck pulling away from our house (and the laundry he left behind) soon became a familiar scene, one that ceased to provoke feelings of acute anxiety.

You see, I learned that he really isn't leaving me. I'm not going to be emotionally abandoned or forever forgotten, as I once thought might be the case. Family bonds, I've decided, have nothing to do with geographic location or dwelling arrangements. They exist in our hearts. We take them with us and remain connected to those we love *wherever* we go.

The nest isn't ever empty. The seasons just change.

Identity Crisis Strikes Grandma

WOULDN'T YOU KNOW IT? Just when I finally shed all (well, almost all) my unwanted pounds, let my hair grow to my waist, and convinced myself I could defy the rules of aging, I received the news. I'm going to be a grandma.

This wasn't supposed to happen. At least not now. Don't I have to be a little more gray, a bit more . . . well, matronly, or at least beyond caring how I look in a pair of jeans? Shouldn't grandchildren accompany retirement instead of a new career? And shouldn't I have finished raising all my children before any of them began reproducing?

Just when I was ready to chuck it all and run off into the woods, pursuing that whole earth-mamma lifestyle, this happens.

My son and his wife have been married for five years. So it isn't as if this should have taken me by surprise. But it did.

I wasn't ready. It was yet another in a series of rites of passage I felt as if I'd been hurled through without warning. (You know, like maybe a warning that my entire concept of who I am was about to be altered in one millisecond.)

It was a Friday night not unlike many others. Ron, my oldest son, and his wife, Julie, were in town for the weekend. My husband, twelve-year-old, and I had agreed to meet them for dinner. As we were seated at our dining table, I observed what appeared to be a party favor forgotten by our table's prior occupants. Being the kind of take-charge person I am, I lifted the object and called to our waiter, "Excuse me. I believe someone left this [glancing at the container in my hand] baby b-o-t-t-l-e—"

Before I could complete the sentence, I noticed a card dangling from the ribbon attached to the top of this frightening messenger of change. In utter terror, I turned it over and read its inscription. Only one word appeared: "Grandma."

In shock, I searched for Ron's eyes. They were hidden behind a video camera. And then I looked at Julie. She was laughing.

But I was crying uncontrollably.

It's funny how a mind can entertain enough thoughts to fill a movie script in the span of one emotional moment. I began thinking about that little child, born to me when I was only seventeen. The one so many feared might become just another statistic. I was thinking about the ripples that advance outward when a pebble is cast into the water. I was saying a prayer of thanks for having lived long enough to have had this experience. Ron's father hadn't been as fortunate.

And then the questions came flooding in. Can I still wear my blue jeans? Does this mean I have to learn to knit? How will this affect my recent decision to become a vegetarian? And perhaps more importantly, will my husband still think of me and Victoria's

Secret in the same tense?

None of those answers came forth readily. (And I'm still assessing that whole Victoria's Secret thing.) So I did what seemed logical to relieve all my fears.

Reaching out, while dodging a protruding camera lens, I shared a family hug . . . with my first grandchild.

The Denim Debate

ACCORDING TO SOME FASHION experts, wearing jeans past a certain age (the woman, not the pants) just isn't done. Now, I'll admit that once I've reached ninety I should probably seek an alternative. Sixteen-inch inseams are going to be hard to find. But until I've shrunk to that extent, I'll probably remain a fan of stretch-fit jeans.

It's not that I'm trying to relive my youth or deny my age (though I'll confess both hold strong appeal). It's just that I've spent a lifetime in denim. From snap-lined toddler coveralls, to skintight hip-huggers, to the relaxed-fit and boot-cut varieties, I've worn them all. So why should I give up on blue jeans before someone invents a style with padded knees?

If you think about it, with armies of baby boomers advancing, can "apple-fit" (with extra abdominal room) be far away?

If you're wondering why jeans hold such timeless allure, let me offer a few insights. First, blue jeans are wardrobe stretchers. When you wear them every day, no one can tell when you're behind with laundry. You can parade about in the same pair of pants for a week and no one will know it. My children, when they were growing up, were especially grateful for this.

Denim trousers are fashion friendly, too. They make life easier for the color-blind or wardrobe challenged. Jeans never have to be matched to, or coordinated with, other garments. Anything will "go" with denim. Early risers who dress in total darkness find this particularly appealing.

Here's another benefit: pet hair won't easily adhere to blue jeans. So if you own a long-haired cat or dog and you wear denim, you won't have to walk around with your pet's imprint stuck to your behind. And when you visit your neighbor, their sofa won't end up looking like Chewbaca sat on it.

If you're size sensitive like me, by merely changing jean styles (say, from misses' regular to ladies' loose-fit) you can increase comfort without advancing to the next numeric size. Let's face it; nobody wants to go from a Misses 8 to a 14 for the sake of closing a zipper. And unlike men, women can't simply lower their waistbands to decrease their circumference.

This brings me to a critical point. It is wholly unfair that men gain their extra weight in the one place where they can best disguise it. A guy can suck in and hold his breath and make twenty pounds disappear, but a woman has no equivalent ability to draw in her hips and thighs. That's why we need our blue jeans.

Denim trousers have double-stitched seams that won't easily split when stressed. And the fabric's thickness disguises any unsightly lumps. By smashing atoms inside cellulite (the only scientific explanation I can offer), jeans hold the power to convert marbled thighs into leaner-looking legs.

I know I share this opinion with the opposite sex because I've often overheard them talking. Many a man has suggested that women past a certain age shouldn't shuck their jeans. You can bet I'll be hanging on to mine.

Right on the Tip of My Tongue

IN EVERY PERSON'S LIFE, if he or she lives long enough, there will be a time when recalling words, names, and facts grows extra challenging. During our forties and fifties, our brains begin to lose neurons, and memory retrieval times lengthen. So technically, I've already started my mental decline. (Though some would argue I must surely have neared completion.) Honestly, some days I can't recollect the topic of my last column.

Midlife makes people slower in some ways and wiser in others. We've learned a great deal we'd like to share with the world; yet, we can't recall what it was or who needed to know about it. We speak to each other in riddles, hand signals, and charades. "Do you know where my thing is?" my spouse often asks me.

Though he's not identified it's his cell phone he's hunting, I intuit what he means. "It's in the . . . that room . . . the one where we sleep," I reply. And he locates the phone immediately, understanding my struggle to recall such infrequently used words as "bedroom."

But occasionally only syllables get rearranged or similar-sounding words interchange themselves for one another. "This is ridiculous," my husband will exclaim in frustration. "At this rate, by next week we'll be breaking out Pictionary so we can communicate with each other."

"Maybe we should start taking some of that ginkgo balboa," I say really serious-like.

"You mean ginkgo *biloba?*" he asks, laughing. "*Balboa* was Sly Stallone's name in that movie, *Rocky.*"

"Whatever," I tell him, annoyed. I didn't give him grief when he couldn't remember the word "porch" that morning. He needn't be acting all high and mighty. A day earlier he'd forgotten the term "dustpan," right after I'd handed him that stick with straw attached to one end.

My search glitch, as I like to call it, accounts for my resistance to participate in computer and board games—especially ones that involve my children. Forget about Trivia Pursuit, I tell them. I'm holding out until they develop a Menopause Edition.

Wheel of Fortune owes much of its appeal to seniors who suffer my affliction. It's not so much that we're fascinated by the contestants and their word clues. We just find inspiration in witnessing how quickly Vanna White can still locate all her letters.

"There's got to be a column idea in here somewhere," I say to my spouse.

"Sure there is," he encourages. "But you better hurry up and write it down before you forget about it."

Fueling
Frustrations

Home Energy-Saving Tips

THE CERTAINTY OF HIGHER energy bills this winter has prompted me to consider stricter conservation efforts. For instance, do I really need to cook? And how often does the laundry actually have to be done? Even vacuuming might not be required as frequently as I'm accustomed to doing it (which is anytime visitors fail to accurately guess the carpet color).

I realize the power companies all provide tips on ways to lower your bills. But think about it; do you truly believe the people who profit from selling energy are going to give you the whole scoop on how to consume less of it? Why, that would be like a lawyer advising you how to draft your own will or a doctor providing you with a list of home remedies. Therefore, I think you'll find my energy saving ideas more meaningful.

Before embarking on a home energy-savings plan, first examine your habits. Are you staying up past 7:00 p.m.? If so, why? Wouldn't twelve hours of sleep leave you feeling better rested?

If you must remain awake after dark, you might think about purchasing one of those head-mounted, battery-powered lights—the kind spelunkers wear. This will allow you to walk around the house without turning on interior lamps. And these gadgets are perfect for reading, too.

Now let's address those kitchen appliances. Do you keep your refrigerator indoors? Refrigerators consume less energy when their exteriors stay cool. Why not relocate your fridge somewhere else for the winter, like maybe your garage or back porch?

And speaking of relocating, how many rooms can you sit in at once? (This is not a trick question aimed at anyone overweight.) There's simply no need to heat the entire house when you're able to enjoy only one part of it at a time. If you'll attach a string or chain to your ceiling vents, you can open and close them off as you come and go. Sure this is a little unsightly. But by adding a toy or feather to these chain pulls, you'll be creating hours of entertainment for your pets.

Have you ever purchased hair sprays or gels that turned your coif into a lethal weapon? Don't throw away those instant hardeners. Use them to caulk your windows, for crying out loud.

Remove half of all your lightbulbs, or simply let them burn out, and don't replace them. Substitute fluorescent lighting for incandescent bulbs in high-use locations, and shut off unused rooms, such as workout areas.

It can be difficult to adjust to changes in average temperatures, so lower your thermostat gradually in increments of one or two degrees. Stop when you can see your breath. To acclimate yourself to a cooler household, layer clothing until you can no longer feed yourself. Then, obviously, you'll need to remove the outermost covering.

Showers are big energy wasters, too. Children, especially, seem to move in slow motion whenever they come into contact with warm water. Here is where a stopwatch comes in handy. Time your kids' showers. It takes thirty seconds to shampoo, fifteen seconds to soap thoroughly, and another minute to scrub and rinse. That's a total of 105 seconds from start to finish. Let your offspring know what's expected, and then shock them with a cold splash anytime they don't heed your two-minute warning.

This brings me back to laundry. You should launder only after your spouse complains coworkers are asking if he wore that same shirt yesterday. Don't worry about the clothes pile. You can always use soiled apparel to block out exterior door drafts. There's a good chance the garments are already on the floor anyway.

Home energy conservation measures can provide considerable advantages for those willing to be creative. I'd share more tips if I had time, but right now I need to retrieve my tea from atop the Sterno.

Self-Checkout Machines Must Go

HAVE YOU EVER BEEN held hostage by a self-checkout machine? I'm talking about one of those stupid mechanical contraptions that has replaced human grocery checkers so that we now have only ourselves to blame for crushed bread.

Normally, I would never attempt to communicate with one of these robotic demons. But only two manned stations were open, each having six to eight patrons in queue, while fourteen empty self-checkout lanes sat enticingly available. "Come hither," the self-scanners beckoned, "and bring me your apples."

Right off, The Evil One asked me to choose a language: Spanish, English, Yiddish, Pig-Latin, etc. Of course, I selected Texan. It then told me to scan my first item, so I did. It was a tube of lipstick.

Beep!

No problem. The tube glided down the conveyor belt, where it promptly lodged between the belt and the metal rollers near the bagging area. I disregarded this slight malfunction and scanned my next item, a pizza the size of a hubcap. (Hey, at least it was *thin crust*.) The box moved along just fine until it hit the lipstick. Then it twisted and jammed itself between the belt and the staging area. That's two for two, I thought. Maybe the next item will shove them along.

I hoisted a six-pack of flavored water above the scanner and waved it back and forth. Nothing. Not even a "thank-you." Tilting the bottles, I tried again. Still nothing. Finally, I noticed a bar code on the inside of one of the plastic containers. Now what? Do I scan it six times or only once? Having never before worked as a grocery clerk, I couldn't be sure. So I scanned it once. This caused The Evil One to go, "Beep!" and then say, "two dollars and twenty-nine cents," which I'm fairly certain was the store's added profit from the fifteen minutes of payroll time I'd already saved them.

The water coasted along until it hit the pizza box. And then Satan yelled, "Remove unwanted items from the belt." Three seconds later, in compliance with ADA regulations, the beast repeated itself a little louder. "Remove unwanted items from the belt!"

But I want *all* of the items on the belt. There *aren't* any unwanted items on the belt!

I lifted the pizza box so the monster would shut up. But now I was standing there holding a pizza and wondering what to do next. Bewildered, I looked around for anyone wearing a name tag. A girl ducked behind a register two aisles away. I swear. She pretended to reload something underneath a counter. A few moments later, I saw her monitoring me as though she might be witnessing a robbery in progress. She seemed to enjoy every second of my frustration. Just to fake her out, I grabbed a bottle of moisturizer and pretended like I was about to slip it into my purse. (Already, Lucifer had lured me over to the Dark Side.) At the last second, I scanned the object and shot her a smirk.

Through the store windows, I noticed the sun had crept low on the horizon. The shoppers that had previously lined the two staffed register lanes were all gone. Probably they were home, their dinners cooked and eaten, their feet propped before their television sets.

Clearly, I am not a good cashier because I am too slow. Feeling inept, I reminded myself that I didn't go to college to become a proficient grocery checker; yet, there I was.

The Evil One said, "Fifty-nine dollars and sixty-seven cents is your total. Please select your payment method."

I stared at the screen, which now contained several rectangles to choose from: Cash, Debit Card, Credit Card, Library Card, or Pawn My Watch. There should have been another option, I've since decided—one that said "Lost Time, Hypertension, and Humiliation."

The Rebate Factor

"I CAN BUY A new computer with all the bells and whistles for less than half what we paid for our old one," my husband enthused. He hadn't bothered to consider the consequences of "the rebate factor."

"What's the price?" I asked.

"With the rebate," he qualified, "it's only six hundred."

I shuddered, realizing what this meant.

Later, I followed my man into the electronics mega-center like a calf being led to slaughter. The trip reminded me of my childhood excursions to the hardware store with my dad—only there were no nails. If I wanted to injure myself, I'd have to venture into the combat zone over by the high definition TVs.

After an hour-long debate over the pros and cons of extended warranties, modems, cables, mouses (mice?), and media packages only Time Warner might need, we'd completed our purchases and were free to leave.

"I'm letting you deal with these rebates," I said, handing a wad of receipts to my hubby. "I *always* have to do them." I acted like the process was something anyone could manage without an advanced degree and antidepressants.

"Fine," he agreed. "I'll do it as soon as we get home."

"Sure you will," I said, snickering. "Just wait until you see what's involved."

He rolled his eyes. "How hard can it be?"

Once he'd unpacked all the boxes, my fellow lamented, "Good grief. There's, like, sixteen rebates here!"

I hid inside my office and pretended to be writing. But eventually I mumbled, "Uh-uh."

A few seconds later he yelled, "How in the heck am I supposed to send the original UPC code to two different places?" I smiled and kept on typing. And then I heard, "These *%#* scissors won't cut through this box! Do we have ANYTHING sharp in this house anywhere?"

"Can't you just use a knife?" I shouted back.

"Yeah, I'm thinking about using one on whoever came up with the idea for these rebates. Where are my glasses? I can't find the flashlight, and I can't read a darn thing on these forms!"

By the time I joined my spouse in the hallway, I was feeling pretty smug. The sight of him sitting there, straddle-legged, hovering over nine receipts with a magnifying glass cracked me up.

This was quite possibly the worst rebate challenge either of us had ever encountered. The breakdown went like this: $50 manufacturer's rebate for the monitor and another $50 for the computer, $150 electronics store rebate for any combination of computer and monitor, $50 electronics store rebate for any computer and printer combo, and another $20 store rebate for any computer package (computer, monitor, and printer).

Each rebate required submittal of a copy of the sales receipt, original UPC code, and the serial and ESN numbers cut from the box.

"How am I supposed to know which one of these is the right number?" my bewildered mate complained. "There are *nine* different bar codes on this box!"

Two days later, after we'd completed and mailed all of the forms, I turned over the sales receipt and read, "For exchange or refund, the product must be returned in its original condition, including the box, UPC bar code, packaging, and all accessories." This computer, I suddenly realized, could turn out to be the most expensive one we've ever owned.

Months passed, and I forgot all about those rebates. While sorting through our mail one day, I noticed what looked like an advertisement from my guy's favorite electronics store. Harrumph! I'm not getting suckered into any more of *their* deals, I thought. I stuck the ad in together with some empty envelopes to be discarded. Then for no reason, I decided to open it. Inside was a rebate check for $150.

I'm thinking maybe I'll use the money to pay for our meds.

Promoting Pasture Pie Power

IF YOU'RE LIKE ME, you're tired of paying high gasoline and home energy prices. So I know you'll be as excited as I was to discover this news; your car, the one you're driving right now, can run on corn. And your house might soon be powered by cow patties!

Now, before you start pulling those little nibblers from the freezer and shoving them into your automobile gas tank, let me explain. Two Dallas energy firms have announced plans to build ethanol plants in the Texas Panhandle. (No, contrary to belief, ethanol plants are not in any way related to tobacco.)

Ethanol is a byproduct of corn. And according to an article I studied for several seconds, today's cars can run on a gasoline mix that can be as much as 85 percent ethanol. (I've no idea where you can buy ethanol or how to mix it with gasoline, so please hold your letter requests.)

But the news keeps getting better. These new ethanol processing plants will be fueled by cow patties! Yes, you read that right—cow chips—which begs an obvious question: how many cow pies does it take to generate a gallon of ethanol? Or better still, how many cattle does it take to excrete enough pasture Frisbees to make a tanker car full of ethanol? And where, exactly, would one locate such a processing plant? Well, in Hereford, Texas, of course—cattle capital of the world, where residents are already used to the smell of fresh manure.

My mind reeled with the many possibilities associated with this new venture. If an ethanol processing plant can be powered by pasture pies, then maybe electric power plants can, too! And if that were true, TXU Electric might soon have to ask for rate hikes based on the increasing cost of manure. They could suddenly begin grazing cattle along utility pole rights-of-way. And given our deregulated markets, we could be flooded with utility firms carrying names like Excrement Electric and Cow Pie Energy.

Immediately, I saw several more problems. First, there'll be a direct impact on the fertilizer industry. Homeowners will have to decide which is more important—lush lawns or the fuel required to mow them. And beef could all but disappear from food store freezers. I mean, why slaughter something that if left alive will fuel your car and generate low-cost energy? Perhaps someone should have researched powering these plants with dog doo instead.

But wait. What about that corn? Folks, I see a serious shortage developing. Think about it. Corn is needed to feed the cows that make the manure that fuels the processing plant that produces the ethanol. Yet the ethanol itself is derived from corn. Corn has suddenly become the key to our whole economy! Entire industries (tortilla, muffin, and even beer) could be crippled by corn shortages. National parklands could be consumed by this crop. Price wars could be waged and legislation enacted to stabilize the forces of supply and demand. Cornmeal lobbyists might become even more powerful than they already are!

Well, if all that happens, most of us will still enjoy major benefits from new forms of renewable energy. We'll be able to drive on chicken feed and power our homes for the price of a few cow pies. So I say, let the chips fall where they may.

What's Driving New Car Buyers?

EVERY AUTUMN, THE NEW car models arrive, and auto dealers cleverly invent all kinds of gimmicks to rid themselves of last year's leftovers. Among some of the incentives offered are free gas (though the ads don't specify if that's petrol, diesel, natural gas, or bodily emissions) and no car payments until next year.

These tricksters don't tell you that those deferred car payments will cost you twice as much six months from now. But hey, *somebody* has to keep the repo man employed.

Today, the playing field has been leveled, and average folks who haven't had an autoworker in the family for two generations can now qualify for "employee pricing." This means you can just waltz right into that showroom and expect those salespeople to treat you as well as they'd deal with any auto factory worker.

It's been rumored that the current employee pricing options are based on those received by Darla Dimwitt. Darla purchased a mustard-toned 2004 compact car last year. After she agreed to finance her vehicle at 15 percent interest for five years, she received a 10-percent discount on the price of the car minus options such as full-size wheels. (Unfortunately,

Darla's boyfriend disappeared with the runabout before she was able to collect on the free car mats.)

Incentives or not, my husband starts contemplating a new car purchase every July. And by September, he's completed his research and is ready to pitch his choice to me. "I think we need to go hybrid," he said this year. Poring over the newspaper sale ads, he added, "But I hear there's a six-month waiting list."

"Shoot," I replied real serious-like. "Who'd want to do that? By then, *next* year's models will be out!"

"Good point," he admitted. Then he went right back to studying the auto section.

I do my best to break my man's new-car fever for as long as possible. And then I refuse to step foot onto any sales lot until all the tire kicking and haggling are over. The way I've got it figured, "dealer prep" and "fleet manager" sound an awful lot like medical terms. Any industry that uses such phrases must want to surgically remove something from me. Probably, that's my wallet.

Yet, there are plenty of valid reasons to buy a new car—better gas mileage and fewer repairs, for instance. And those huge rebates are often the only way to pay for last year's holiday purchases before this year's kick in.

Periodically, drivers of neutral-painted cars are forced to replace their vehicles because they lose them. On any given Sunday night, at least a dozen white sedans can be found in otherwise empty mall parking lots. Tragically, those autos have been abandoned by owners who simply gave up on ever finding them again. Like Darla, these future buyers will gravitate toward Dijon-colored cars.

Still, some individuals think they can steer their way to status. So every time they get a salary increase, they ratchet up their transportation. (The psychological term for this is the "Na-na-na-na-na, I'm driv-ing a Jag-uar" syndrome.) You'll see these same people standing in line at McDonald's paying for their Happy Meals with their Visa cards.

Finally, there are those like my hubby who can't stand the idea of owning an outdated set of wheels. Unfortunately, this trendsetter mentality doesn't carry over to his closet. His wardrobe is vintage '80s.

So don't be surprised if you see my guy driving around in something hip and new. When you spot him, please do me a favor. Ask him if that jacket he's wearing is an authentic Members Only.

Twelve-Step Support for Pickup Truck Owners

WITH GASOLINE PRICES SPIRALING higher every day, I've been thinking a lot about pickup trucks. Studying the roadways causes me to wonder if gas guzzling might be a local pastime. The compact cars and sedans of yesterday no longer dominate our streets. Now, it seems that everyone drives a fuel-hogging truck or an SUV.

I can't help wondering; at what gas price will pickup truck and SUV owners be forced to trade their vehicles for something more along the line of, say, a Mini Cooper? Or better still, use their John Deere riding lawn mowers for local transportation? (Maybe even hook up one of those garden trailers to tote the kids.)

I know I'm in Texas where essentially only two types of people exist: those who own a pickup truck, and those who need one. But I've always been a member of the latter camp because, given the choices, I'd rather be a borrower than a lender. It didn't take me long to figure out that, when I needed a truck, I could rent one from a home improvement store (and use their gas) for $19.99/hour. No special insurance required. No expensive tires to buy. No gas mileage concerns. And, frankly, no one who'd be inclined to ask me to help them move during weekends.

Now, I realize that construction contractors can't pull a trailer with a Toyota Prius, and families with children have lifestyle challenges that prevent them from converting to gas-efficient autos. You can't easily force three children, two Game Boys, a personal DVD player, four movies, a small ice cooler, and a twenty-piece bucket of chicken into a Volkswagen Jetta. Maybe soon they'll come out with a hybrid vehicle that will run on snack cake wrappers and juice box and Happy Meal containers. Probably some big wheel at McDonald's already has authorized and funded the research.

Personally, I'm waiting for the hybrid car that'll go fifty miles on a bundle of wire coat hangers or a loaf of moldy sandwich bread. If they ever develop an automobile that runs on recycled paper, I'll be fueled for life. In fact, I've been stockpiling resources for years.

A fellow I know wants a flashy sports car that will climb from zero to eighty in sixty seconds, one that can be rocketed by either beard clippings or intestinal gas.

But until these alternative fuels can be implemented (or until folks take their riding lawn mowers out into the streets), maybe someone ought to start a support group for gas guzzlers, a sort of twelve-step organization for truck owners, if you will. These individuals surely could use a place to process their pain.

If you need a sponsor, you can easily locate me because I'm often steering a pickup that displays a big blue sign. There's an ad on the driver's side door that reads, "Rent me for just $19.99."

In Search of the Average Household

HEATING AND COOLING BILLS are expected to skyrocket by as much as 90 percent in the coming months. Because of this, journalists suggest that the average electric bill will run about $175 per month. Using that same 90-percent forecast, however, ours will eclipse the cost of my granddaughter's entire Barbie collection (including Ken and Kelly).

This causes me to wonder. Who are these "average" people anyway? I don't know about you, but I'm tired of constantly being compared to someone I can't identify. Who's responsible for these impossible-to-achieve living standards? Good grief. My dry-cleaning expenses exceed what the average American shells out annually for clothing (roughly $400). How is that possible? Are they nudists or what?

The standard household gets fewer miles out of their car each year than I get out of my credit cards. And the only way I could match the average health care premium ($226 per month) would be to eliminate everyone on our plan except maybe the cat.

The typical Texan spends $153 per month on gasoline and substantially less on auto insurance. And neither their property taxes nor their holiday purchases force them to take out a home equity loan. Obviously, they're driving a golf cart, living in a travel trailer, and frequenting garage sales.

In search of elusive and occasionally fictitious journalistic sources, I recently located the culprit behind these irksome statistics—Robert Paul and Betty Joanne Average.

Yes, that's right. Robert and Betty, a retired couple living in South Texas, signed up for MediaShortcuts.com. In doing so, they became instant references for thousands of writers who are either too lazy or underpaid to make long distance phone calls. Do you need a statistic about the "Average" household? Just e-mail Robert and Betty Joanne.

Because I have free long distance service on my cell phone, I contacted Mr. and Mrs. Average. Here's what I learned during an interview with them:

I'm curious about how you keep your utility bills so low. Exactly how large is your home?

Robert: We've got over a thousand square feet, about twelve-hundred all together. It's a concrete block and stucco one-story, which really helps. And I put in one of those solar-powered hot water heaters, too.

Betty: (Giggling) We also shower together sometimes.

Okay. I understand you've taken an economical and efficient approach to home construction and water conservation, but how about your auto-related expenses?

Betty: Well, we only have the one car because I never learned how to drive.

Robert: I'm still driving my old El Camino. Bought her new, right off the showroom floor, back in 1987. Runs like a top. And we don't need much insurance out here because the only road hazard in these parts is the four-legged kind.

Well, that explains quite a bit. But I'd like to know how you keep those holiday purchases under $600 every year.

Betty: Oh, that's easy. Robert spends so much time hunting deer, turkey, and wild hogs in the fall that I get a little stir crazy. So I pull out my sewing machine to pass the time. I make a lot of our gift items. Last year, I made Robert a set of sweats out of camo-print polar fleece, but picking him free of all those cockleburs after he wore them sure wasn't something I'd counted on.

Well, thank you both. You've been a big help.

There you have it, folks. The next time you catch yourself wondering why your expenses seem out of whack with the average household's, don't be fooled by semantics. "Average" doesn't necessarily mean "typical."

Next, I'm going to track down Mr. and Mrs. *Standard*.

Texas Trouble

Jalapeño Hazards

AT FIRST GLANCE, JALAPEÑO peppers might appear innocuous. However, bite into one, and you'll feel as though you've emptied a thousand Red Hots into your mouth. And if the juice should touch your lips, you'll swear you've been sprayed with mace.

Despite this, jalapeños are an essential ingredient in Tex-Mex cuisine. My hot sauce recipe is no exception. One day, though, these peppers punched up more than my salsa.

It was a sizzling day in August, on an afternoon so hot that squirrels refused to scamper and cicadas agreed to silence. My son Ron, his wife Julie, and the dog they affectionately call my "grandpuppy" had just arrived from out of town. Initially, I thought our swimming pool might be responsible for their impromptu visit, but soon I realized they'd simply run out of hot sauce.

I said, "I'll make some for you, if you agree to help me." Then I held open my refrigerator door for several minutes, letting the chilled air dry my damp face. "Let me see," I said, peering inside. "I've got tomatoes, cilantro, Spanish onions, bell peppers, and, of course, these," I said, handing a bag of jalapeño peppers to Ron. "*You* can seed them."

He seated himself at the kitchen table, and asked, "What do you mean? Seed?"

"I mean cut them lengthwise and scrape out all the seeds." Did he need me to say this in Pig Latin? I warned him to be careful. "You don't want to get any of that juice on you. *Anywhere*."

Ron gave me a look that suggested maybe I'd regressed a full twenty years. "I think I can handle it, Mom." He grabbed a serrated knife and sawed away.

I thought to myself, he might be a police officer but he doesn't know *everything*. "Don't rub your eyes, whatever you do," I insisted.

"Got it," he said with a smirk.

Julie agreed she'd peel the tomatoes if I'd chop the onions and cilantro. As the three of us butchered produce, an odoriferous cloud formed inside the kitchen. This made our eyes water and the dog gasp for breath, so we opened a door.

Our red and green soup had to simmer first, then boil for thirty minutes. Waiting, I cleaned the aftermath of what looked like a vegetable massacre. I'd just begun rinsing my hands when my mother phoned.

"What are you doing?" she asked.

"Making hot sauce," I said. "Ron and Julie are here."

"Hot sauce! What are you going to do with *that?*"

Mom doesn't understand voluntary combustion. She's the only one in our family who won't consume spicy foods. "Well, I thought we might *eat* it," I said, laughing. Then I scanned the room for Ron, hoping he might be nearby and willing to rescue me from this inquisition. Maybe he'd want to say "hi" to his grandmother, but he'd gone to the restroom.

Mom had completed her dietary critique when I heard Ron race into the kitchen. He looked as if he'd been hit with a branding iron, bouncing first on one foot and then the other. With one hand, he firmly clasped his "manhood."

I pulled free of the phone receiver and mouthed, "What's wrong with you?"

He shouted back, "I'm on F-I-R-E! Quick! What do you put on a jalapeño burn?"

Confused, I asked, "Where's the burn?"

"On my John-son!"

Mom hollered through the receiver, "*What* did he just say?"

I ignored the question. "How did you get jalapeño juice on *that?*" I inquired not really wanting to know.

"He got juice on his privates?" Mom asked.

I searched the room for Julie and found her standing to my right. She stared at her husband and giggled.

"Is ANYBODY going to give me something here?" cried Ron.

From the refrigerator I retrieved a tub of margarine. "Here. Take this and rub some on . . . you know," I said, handing him the spread. "Just don't *dip!*"

"Tell him to pour milk on it," Mom instructed.

I repeated this to Julie. She grabbed a carton and chased after him.

Now, I'd be lying if I said I haven't savored this moment. Come to think of it, that hot sauce was the best I've ever made!

When It Hits the Fan

TEENAGERS HAVE EVERY REASON to be lethargic. They're undergoing a transformation from precious children to punishing reminders of their parents' worst traits. And it takes a lot of food to fuel that leap. That's why they often appear listless and, yes, possibly deaf. But don't be fooled; they hear you. It's just that they can't respond to your commands. They're conserving their physical energy so they can eat more.

Having suffered through four teenagers, three of them at once, I should be qualified for induction into the Abused Domestic Servant Survivors' Hall of Fame. At a minimum, I ought to receive a discount on Prozac.

My teens practiced their economies of movements in ways guaranteed to spike anyone's blood pressure. I'd come home from work to find a kitchen that looked as if it had been ransacked by burglars, ones possibly searching for hidden silver. Every cabinet door had been thrown wide and left open. Drawers protruded out at half-tilt, threatening to empty their contents at any second. On the countertop, a loaf of bread spilled from its plastic encasing, and cheese slice wrappers dotted and stuck to the tile surface.

For extra ambiance, I'd discover empty boxes of crackers, cereals, and cookies inside the pantry where one of the slothful youths had removed the final morsel.

Condiment jars were never to be trusted at our house. My kids repeatedly set them back into the refrigerator without first tightening the lids. This made life fairly interesting when I forgot and removed items like pickles from the fridge.

One Saturday afternoon, the family had gathered around the kitchen table for a feast of hamburgers. And since I'm a true Texan and don't eat mustard on mine, I'd forgotten to set any out for my Yankee husband.

"Get me the hot mustard," he called out to our daughter Laura. She was standing in front of the refrigerator, looking like she'd gone into another one of her hypnotic trances.

"Okay," she said, her hearing suddenly restored.

Now, I should first explain that the fridge was only a few steps away and that a ceiling fan hung directly above our dinette. Also, our kitchen resembled a sanitarium in more ways than one. Everything inside it was white, including the cabinets, floors, appliances, and countertops.

Right when Laura started for the table with the jar of Dijon, its lid broke free from a crusty hold. The container sailed to the ground at some incalculable speed that seemed achievable only by jet propulsion.

Glass exploded onto the floor with such force that it launched a surge of yellow some six feet into the air. (I am not exaggerating about this.) From there, the condiment splattered onto the ceiling fan—which happened to be running at high speed—and spun around the kitchen, turning the room into what looked like a Jackson Pollock painting.

I lurched for the switch to kill the dastardly propeller while everyone else went into suspended animation. Frozen in place, Laura's mouth gaped as she held absentmindedly to the jar lid.

The gusher had formed a swirl on the ceiling above us. And every cabinet, appliance, and door was now sprinkle-seasoned. It looked as if a bomb had exploded in a Heinz factory.

My husband was the first to speak. "It b-u-r-n-s," he uttered to no one in particular.

I glanced up from dabbing at the cabinetry to study his face while the children howled. On their father's forehead, which I might add is rather prominent, sat a dollop of what he'd initially requested for his burger. He made no move to rid himself of the Cyclops marking on his noggin.

Now, if I were hit with a burning blob of sandwich spread, I doubt I'd wait for someone to notice. I'd jump up, grab something, and wipe it off. That leads me to think the mustard might launch a good ways from the jar—but the seeds seldom fall far from the sprig.

Designer Dog

THE BLUE LACY IS now the official state dog breed of Texas. I'm sharing this important information with you because, as far as I know, this news escaped headlines. Thus, it's entirely possible you have no idea what a Blue Lacy is or why Texas needed an official state dog. Let me assure you, I can answer one of these questions.

I must first confess that my exposure to the Blue Lacy breed is limited to the dog my son acquired last spring. After his Benji-looking companion of twelve years died, he and his family purchased what I like to call "one of them designer dogs." When he phoned to tell me about his new puppy, his voice was filled with pride. "This dog is great with children," he said, "and it'll do the work of five cowboys!"

Now my son Ron lives in a subdivision and owns no livestock, so I kind of wondered about his cowboy comment. "What do you mean?" I asked.

"He's a herding animal that instinctively knows what to do," Ron explained. I could see how this might be beneficial for anyone who has children. "Mom, this dog cost me three *hundred* dollars!" he added. Now, I was thoroughly impressed. I wouldn't have thought any of my children knew how to save that much money.

I turned to the Internet to learn more about our new family member. There I discovered that the Blue Lacy is a rare class of dog that's native to Texas. Four brothers (George, Ewin, Frank, and Harry Lacy) developed this breed from greyhound, scent hound, and coyote stock. The animal often carries a blue gene that gives its coat a gun metal color and encourages dumb dog names like "Levi."

Such an unusual pet deserves a special name.

Ron calls his dog Tex.

When I first met Tex, he was a three-month-old cuddly ball of velvet. He trotted right up to me with his tail wagging and his little tongue hanging out of his mouth. Then he stopped, straddled my sandals, and peed.

Right off I could see this dog was different, but I didn't know the extent of his novelty. Tex, as it turns out, will eat just about anything. In the beginning, he thrived on fresh-baked chocolate chip cookies stolen from the kitchen countertop. Then he advanced to shop rags, my granddaughter's swimsuit, and my grandson's disposable diapers. And his unexpected appetite didn't end there.

Soon my granddaughter reported finding colorful dog doo, which confirmed her suspicions about missing crayons. Tex had also eaten her Polly Pocket doll's apparel. We were sure of this when Tex's *deposits* suddenly appeared fully accessorized by miniature purses and shoes.

Whatever Tex doesn't eat, he buries. Not only can he replace five cowboys, but he can apparently do the work of two backhoes. After my daughter-in-law's garden gloves disappeared, I understood why the Blue Lacy makes a good search and rescue animal. In her backyard she found one glove finger pointing heavenward from the lawn. Upon excavation, both garden mitts were recovered from where Tex had entombed them.

"Oh, yeah, he does this all the time," said my daughter-in-law. "We never know where the kids' stuffed animals will turn up. He steals them, buries them, then digs them up later and returns them," she recounted.

Tex has now reached his full height, which enables him to find entertainment in unlikely places—like the master bathroom. Recently, he rounded the hallway and entered the living room with Ron's toothbrush hanging from one jaw.

Maybe there's something to this designer dog stuff after all. I mean, some people have to wrestle their dogs to brush their teeth. But Tex can brush his own! It's obvious why a dog like that would impress our state legislature.

Hunting Dough during Dove Season

EACH YEAR IN SEPTEMBER, a mysterious urge seizes some Texans (most of whom are men). An internal call, one I've obviously never heard, drives these people from their air-conditioned homes and out into the blazing heat. Dressed like Special Ops troops, they journey to faraway fields to find the universal symbol of peace—the dove—and promptly shoot it.

If you can think of any explanation for this bizarre behavior, please write and share it with me. Otherwise, I'm left to draw my own possibly misinformed conclusions. I have no real experience with this sport because the only hunting my husband does this time of year takes place on new car dealer lots.

But a lack of experience has never prevented me from waging an opinion. So here's my theory about the origins of dove hunting. Maybe the guy who invented the slingshot felt the need to target practice on something. (Boredom can be such a destructive force.) And the spots on a mourning dove's back just looked enticing. For historical reference, this would have occurred sometime around the year 1000 BBB (Before Beer Bottles).

Anyway, like I was saying, I can't tell you why we're still taking aim at doves today. If you think about it, dove hunting equates to a whole lot of time, effort, and expense for something that basically tastes like chicken.

These harmless birds don't compete with man in any way, and unlike their larger cousin, the pigeon, they've never once been accused of overthrowing anyone's shopping center management.

Yet, some people might have a distasteful view of the cooing, monogamous dove. I mean, who wants to hear that repetitious calling to a wayward mate so early in the morning? And what can be made of a male bird that sits on a nest all day feeding its young? Such an anomaly could challenge some folks' ideas of gender roles.

But aside from any satisfaction derived from knocking off a few henpecked husbands (the winged ones, that is), I find no discernable reason for this sport.

From a financial standpoint, a meal of grilled dove will cost you more than dinner at The Ritz. A single (or married) dove yields only one ounce of meat, all of it dark. This means that to feed a family of four, a hunter would have to bag at least two dozen fowl. And depending on the gunner's thirst quencher of choice, that could take anywhere from two days to several seasons.

Texas Parks and Wildlife estimates that five million dove are bagged annually in Texas. Yet statewide, hunters spend $5-10 million on shotgun shells during dove season. So for every dove killed, at least one to two dollars' worth of ammo has been purchased. And the expenses don't stop there.

First, there's the 20-gauge shotgun. Then, there's the apparel that distinguishes hunters from the rest of us who dress to avoid being accidentally shot. Add in land use and license fees, any overnight stays, and gasoline expenses, and those birds' feet might as well be banded with platinum. Tally all that with the related beverage expenses, and the total price per pound of dove meat exceeds the cost of college tuition (including books).

Of course, my husband's hobby during early fall isn't exactly cheap. There's only one short showroom step between a test drive and a new car purchase, and often he takes it. That's why during dove season, we'll be eating chicken.

Texas Chain Saw Adventure

MY HUSBAND AND I decided to buy property in the Texas Hill Country for our future retirement. We'd vacationed several times in the Fredericksburg, Bandera, and Medina areas and knew this region offered the wildlife, vistas, and serenity we'd longed for in Dallas. So we set out in search of the ideal plot of land, one that would offer us the most "bang for the buck," and I don't mean male deer.

Peggy Jeffers, at Texas Rose Realty, was eager to help. Her expertise led us to what seemed like the ideal lot: one that offered panoramic hilltop views somewhat obscured by trees. The land, which had once been part of a working ranch, was overgrown from years of cedar having taken its course. Through its middle, a dense thicket prevented any chance of human penetration; that is, unless one doesn't mind suffering lacerations, puncture wounds, and gouged eyeballs. We bought the four-acre tract before we'd fully determined its potential.

Being more or less city slickers, we deemed ourselves industrious and educated enough to learn how to clear a cedar brake. After all, we'd previously trimmed six massive oaks in our backyard. Through a lifetime of landscape adventures, my husband Jim certainly knew how to wield a chain saw. We weren't arborists. But how difficult could it be to take out a few, okay, maybe a bunch of trees?

Once we'd finalized the sale, we arrived at the property enthusiastic and armed for the cedar challenge. From a local home improvement store, Jim had purchased a new heavy-duty chain saw that included a 20-inch blade and a safety guard. And he still had that glazed-over look in his eyes (one that warned his body had been possessed by some crazed warrior spirit) when he fired it up. The gas-powered engine roared like a panther. "Oh, Ba-by," he said into the air.

Now, any thinking person would have recognized that trouble awaited. But I didn't.

I should explain first that we were miles (I had no idea how many) from the nearest medical emergency center, and that I'm one of those wimpy types who can faint at the sight of blood. Furthermore, my vision had been hampered on this day because I'd accidentally left home without my eyeglasses. To make matters worse, we were in deer country. Around any bend, I might encounter Bambi straddling the road's center stripe. Without my lenses, I'd be lucky to navigate a curve after dark, much less avoid any kamikaze critters. Thus, I had no intention of driving.

The sun had already melted over the hilltops when we decided to quit working. I gathered stray branches and plumes of cedar, wondering each time I crooked my body how I'd find the energy to stretch upright again. In the distance, I heard the chain saw growl one last time and Jim shout, "Whoa!"

I spun and zeroed in on my mate. He jutted out one leg, displaying his newly-frayed pants. "I caught my jeans," he said with a chuckle. "Good thing I have fast reflexes."

Even I knew better than to believe him. "Ohmigod," I cried. "Are you sure you didn't cut yourself?"

"No. I don't think so," he said. Then he peeked through a gaping hole in the fabric encasing his thigh. "Uh, well, maybe I did."

"How badly?" I asked, reminding myself to breathe.

"I'll be okay," he said. "It's just a minor wound." He danced close enough for me to witness his blood-stained jeans.

"Let me see," I demanded. I had to know whether to search for a tourniquet or dial 9–1–1.

An emergency operator said the nearest hospital was in San Antonio, some forty-five minutes away. The dispatcher couldn't provide me directions, but she asked if I'd like her to send an ambulance to assist me. I didn't know how long that might take, so I said no. Somehow, I'd find a doctor.

"I'm okay. Really. I can drive," Jim said when he remembered I couldn't see in the dark. "It's already coagulating," he insisted.

My head swooned; my stomach roiled. Like a traffic cop, I motioned with one hand for him to stop talking. The thought of blood and the image of his mangled flesh only heightened my condition. I could tell I was seconds away from "lights-out."

Snaking along winding lanes in total darkness, I strained to follow the roadway. The night air rushing through my lowered window briskly whipped me back to full alert.

In Boerne, I made a quick stop that connected me with a stranger. The kind man provided the directions I needed, and then he sent me on my way with some bottled water and a few words of encouragement. "It's only eighteen more miles," he said. "And it looks like your husband will be all right. He just needs some stitches."

At North Central Baptist Hospital, Jim received prompt attention. A few sutures, a tetanus shot, and some antibiotics restored all but his mood. "Does it hurt?" a nurse asked.

"Only my pride," he admitted.

By the next morning, my spouse appeared to have made a full recovery. In his best John Wayne voice, he said, "I'm going back out there to do some more work." If I'd had my way, the nose of our car would have been pointed due north towards Dallas. But something akin to retaliation caused us to return to the accident scene. My taskmaster mate worked his chain saw so hard that day that it blew its own belt.

Our friends, James and Cherry Jones, stopped by to examine our progress and Jim's injuries. Being native Hill Country folk, they were quick to point out how far in over our heads we might be. "Do you guys have a shotgun out here?" James asked, presumably trying to scare me.

"What would we need a shotgun for?" I retorted. "Who's going to bother us here?" I was thinking how a gun would only give Jim another chance to hurt himself, maybe shoot his toes off or something worse.

"It's not who . . . but what," said James. "If a wild pig comes through these woods, you're going to need something to slow it down with. And come spring, by the way, you'd better be ready for rattlesnakes," he warned. I was still processing all this when he mentioned stinging scorpions and deadly spiders, too. "Oh, yeah, and that over there sure looks like poison ivy," he said pointing to a clump of vines I'd bare-handedly pawed all afternoon.

I guess the Hill Country offers more than the scenic views and vast sunsets for which it is famous. There's a good deal here that these two city dwellers initially overlooked. Yes, there are beauty and wildlife, unspoiled land, and friendly people. But there are also countless ways for us to harm ourselves or hone our survival skills. In time, I hope we'll fully understand our future homeland. Until then, please be on the lookout for an ashen-faced woman who's driving erratically. Chances are good that she's in a blind search for the nearest emergency center.

Dangerous Detours

What Moms Really Want

AROUND MOTHER'S DAY EVERY year, mailboxes and newspapers are packed with catalogs and sales brochures recommending gifts for the woman whose duty it is to remember (and share with others) your most embarrassing moments—Mom. The ads hawk everything from chunky jewelry suitable for the Gen-X crowd, to cameras that can only be operated by MIT graduates, to shoes designed to guarantee today's podiatrists will never run out of patients. Like many, I study these marketed products and wonder. Whose mom truly wants these items?

Being a mother myself, I'd like to offer a few counter-suggestions. Moms REALLY want:

• To be visited for no reason whatsoever.

• To be asked for family recipes and love and marriage advice.

• To have their children demonstrate healthy attitudes toward others.

• To see that they've raised resilient and self-sufficient progeny.

• To be acknowledged for the things they've done right and forgiven for what they've done wrong.

- To know that they can always trust their children.

- To receive unlimited hugs and kisses.

- To feel that the maternal bond is everlasting and that it flows both ways.

- To be assured that any offspring who becomes a writer will suffer selective memory.

Okay, I'll admit it. That last one I sort of threw in there for myself.

In honor of Mother's Day, I'd like to pay tribute to one of my favorite poems, by Jenny Joseph, about a woman who declares her right to wear purple when she's old. You might say that Ms. Joseph's well-known work inspired the following:

When I'm an old woman, I shall NOT wear pantyhose. Instead, I will use these vile, unnaturally-colored leggings to suspend onions from a hook inside my pantry. And I shall throw away my girdle and swear I haven't seen it and that I don't know where it is. I shall let my breasts travel as far south as they wish and never again choose underwire. When I'm an old woman, I will eat lemon drops all day and say I've no money for Metamucil. I'll spend my retirement monies on beach vacations, and I'll sing Jimmy Buffet songs loud enough for all to hear. When I'm an old woman, I shall feed stray animals and discourage unwanted overnight guests. And I will refuse to dye my hair purple, shave my legs, or purchase shoes that aren't shaped like real feet.

Hurricane Tests

HAVE YOU EVER NOTICED that as our parents age, they increasingly test our devotion? First, they retire and move to some foreign place like Weeki Wachee just to see if we can still find them. From there, they call us periodically to tell us not to worry (which actually means they hope that, due to their new distance, we'll be incapacitated with grief). Whenever we contact them, they rarely let us in on anything that isn't guaranteed to stimulate immediate distress. My mother likes to share things like, "I'm cutting my heart medication into quarters to make it go further." Through some strange reversal of habits, she's begun ignoring doctors' advice and actively courting danger.

Three years ago, Mom retired and moved to Florida—lightning capital of the US. She wasn't afraid of storms, and I guess she figured two billion alligators couldn't be wrong. To further elevate my concerns, she refuses to evacuate for hurricanes.

"We'll be okay," Mom recently assured me as a major hurricane tracked her direction. "The eye is supposed to make landfall seventy miles from here." The way she said this, you'd have thought we were discussing the probability of the sun's collision with Earth.

"Why won't you come visit me and wait this thing out?" I pleaded, knowing fully well that she'd refuse. She'd never let me off that easy.

"My back hurts," she said. "I don't want to ride that far in a car."

Boarding a plane was out of the question. I might just as well ask her to skateboard cross-country.

When we next spoke, Mom laughed at the urgency in my voice. (It was the same sinister laugh that had escaped her when she'd told me how, when I was a child, I'd nearly strangled between two crib rails.) "We'll be all right," she insisted. "Stop worrying. We've got plywood over the windows."

Now, you have to understand that my mother's idea of disaster preparedness is having a camp stove, some honey buns, instant coffee, and one of those battery-operated mister fans (no larger than a deodorant stick) on hand.

"What have you done to prepare for power failure?" I asked.

"We've got a deck of cards and a cell phone," she said, emphasizing the cards. Clearly, the loss of television programming was her most immediate concern. The cards were a substitute, I guess, for *The Price Is Right* and *All My Children*.

"That's nice, Mom. I imagine you can play a wicked game of 52-card Pick Up in 160-mile-an-hour winds," I wanted to tell her. But instead I asked, "Do you have a generator? Have you got water?"

"No. We don't have a generator."

"But it's *hot* there." I pressed on. "What'll you do when the air-conditioning goes out?"

"Oh, I guess we'll open the windows," she said, presumably to see if I was paying attention. Then she added, "After the wind stops, of course."

The next night, the hurricane cut a swath through Florida, its eye passing less than one-hundred miles from Mom's house. We spoke by phone as it came ashore, and then remained online with each other for sometime thereafter.

At 2:00 a.m., when the winds were approaching 60 mph, Mom said, "I can hear noises and banging outside, but I can't see anything because of the plywood." My stomach knotted. I had the same sick feeling I get when watching one of those National Geographic programs about nature—the ones that show some predator sneaking up on an unsuspecting bunny.

An hour later, the wind speeds now gusting to 90 mph, Mom wrote in an e-mail that (surprise!) she was eating a honey bun. Then the hurricane eye made landfall and delivered a temporary reprieve, so I went to bed and slept for a couple hours. But first I asked God to protect Mom from the worst—her apparent lack of valid reasoning.

I was again awake by 5:45 a.m. and watching the Weather Channel. Scenes of collapsed bridges and flooded roadways dominated the air waves. I tried to call Mom, but all the phone lines in her area were jammed. Eventually, she contacted me by cell phone. As she relayed the damage, her phone's battery began to die.

"Quick, Mom, plug in the charger," I blurted.

"I can't," she said. "There's no power in the house."

"Plug it into your car charger then."

"I would, but I don't have one."

"What brand is it? What model? What does it look like?" I fired back.

Faintly, I heard Mom say, ". . . Nokia . . .," then nothing.

The rest of that day I researched cell phone models and chargers.

I made calls, visited stores, and at last found a "universal" charger that operates from an automobile cigarette lighter. Hurrying against the clock, I carried a box containing the charger, an assortment of batteries, and a few canned goods to a local shipper.

When Mom received her package the next morning, she immediately called to thank me. "Are you talking to me from the car?" I asked, inflated with self-pride. Surely, I reasoned, I'd passed Mom's latest test. Maybe I'd proven, once and for all, the extent of my love.

"No, I'm in the house," she said matter-of-factly. "I got the power back this morning."

Who was she kidding? We both knew the truth. Mothers don't ever lose their power.

Abnormal Dad's Day

EVERY YEAR, I HAVE a difficult time finding a suitable Father's Day card for my dad. Phrases like "World's Best Dad" and "You're Number 1" (as opposed to number 2?) seem like unverifiable boasts that convey little. Despite my best intentions, I generally settle for something equally unoriginal like, "Have a Happy Father's Day." I've looked but can't find a card that reads, "Have an inspiring afternoon mixing concrete!" or "Bon Voyage this Father's Day!"

You see, my dad has a mysterious and obsessive relationship with adventure travel and Kwikcrete. In fact, cement is required to hold him in one place for more than a few days. When he's exhausted every opportunity to pour concrete footers, slabs, or foundations, he'll embark on some cross-country mission to find ghost towns or what's left of Old Route 66.

"I never want to be accused of being normal," Dad proudly offers when I suggest he's acting weird. And so far, to the best of knowledge, no one has classified him as such.

One summer when I was nineteen, my father, in Biblical fashion, built a wooden boat. Though the vessel wouldn't hold two of every creature, it was large enough to carry him and all four of his children to their potential deaths. Mom, having shared a longer history with Dad and therefore being less of a believer, had been left behind.

By Father's Day, he'd completed construction of his first (and, I might add, last) human-propelled water vessel, so Dad suggested a family afternoon outing. Think *Gilligan's Island*. A three-hour tour this was to have been. Using his Corps of Engineers map, Dad plotted a course along the Sabine River, one he felt sure we could easily oar before nightfall. He gave Mom instructions to drop us off at one point and to park his car and trailer at another two miles downstream where we were supposed to exit. But when we didn't show up by dark, Mom had to send a rescue team to find us.

Dad's map, possibly his math, and certainly his foresight had been grossly inaccurate. The distance we'd tried first to row and then later to hike had exceeded thirteen miles. We'd encountered a log jam at about the two-mile mark, so we'd wandered in the woods all night. Search crews finally located us the following morning. But that's another story.

My point is this: I don't have one of those Ward Cleaver kind of fathers. Mine has always been more like Chevy Chase's character, Clark Griswold, in *Christmas Vacation*. He means well, but his plans often go astray and become a calamity of sorts.

Occasionally, Dad will stare at the ceiling and remark, "I wonder if my boat's still down there somewhere." Whenever he says this, I immediately try to think of someplace, any place, that I might need another concrete piling or footer.

This year, I'll let my column serve as my Father's Day card. I've got all the concrete I need right now, so Dad has set out on another river trip (in a larger boat and deeper waters this time). And though I'll miss him on Father's Day, I'm kind of glad he didn't ask me to go with him.

Fright Night: Blame It on the Irish

IT'S TIME YOU KNEW the truth about our nation's second most commercial holiday—Halloween. I'm the perfect person to explain this because, well, I'm Irish.

Our story begins with "my people," those of Celtic origin (and short, stumpy stature) who centuries ago celebrated their new year on November 1. When you think of the revelry surrounding our current New Year's Eve, it's immediately apparent why the Celts dressed up on October 31st. However, they didn't have sequins and tuxedos, so they had to make do with animal heads and skins instead. Thus, the night before November 1 was typically a disturbing time for Irish setters.

Anyway, Christianity influenced these pagans to replace their much celebrated "festival of the dead" with the more palatable All Hallows Eve. This resulted in a branching out of traditional costumes to include angels and other religious figures, such as Yoda. In one of the earliest known attempts at political correctness, people disguised as devils, demons, and witches were permitted to commingle with their Christian counterparts.

Harvested foods played a role in these celebrations, too. But since pumpkins weren't then readily available in the UK, they had to make do with vegetables like rutabagas.

When I first learned that my ancestors had carved up turnips for jack-o-lanterns, I was astounded. That is, until I remembered that leprechauns have really small hands. Besides, somebody had to invent a use for ugly produce.

The Celts got so carried away with root crops that they ended up creating a potato famine. The number of potatoes that starved has never been precisely documented. But it's a widely held belief that this shortage spawned what later became the plastic version of Mr. Potato Head.

The Potato Famine of 1846 also caused a mass exodus of Irish immigrants to the US. These foreign residents brought along with them the customs of our current Halloween, and the idea for cereals like Lucky Charms. Additionally, they inspired such key marketing concepts as the Keebler elves.

By the early 1900s, Americans had decided to convert Halloween to a more family- and community-centered holiday. And what could be more patriotic and family-centered than shopping and candy? If you think there's a coincidence between this timeline and the fact that Milton Hershey began mass producing his chocolate bars in 1900, then you might want to check with the government. Possibly your IQ could make you eligible for disability benefits.

From there, companies like Hallmark and Spencer's Gifts got into the act. What started off as a simple Celtic New Year's Eve celebration became the second largest retail holiday in the US. It wouldn't surprise me to learn that when consumer confidence is polled, one of the primary questions asked is, "How much do you plan to spend on Halloween purchases this year?" I even bet that Mexico's pumpkin exports to North America produced the need for NAFTA. Otherwise, we might all be carving turnips.

By now, you understand the significant contributions made by my heritage. The Irish are responsible for Halloween and much of our nation's economy. Quite possibly you thought we'd only brought you St. Patrick's Day and green beer, but we're a motley bunch with an often wicked sense of truth. So there you have it. "Trick or treat."

Thanksgiving Migration

THROUGH A PROCESS THAT resembles the way whales know to migrate or bees select a queen, my family decides where to go for their Thanksgiving Day feast. Because she lived in the country and had a leg up on everybody else, my grandmother held our family assembly title for more than four decades. But the matron with this honor didn't demand it. She earned the privilege over a lengthy time and a hot stove and maybe somewhat by default. Nobody else found it invigorating to cook for fifteen. And it was impossible for the rest of us to duplicate her cornbread dressing.

But after she turned eighty, Grandma passed the turkey platter to the next generation. And as in politics, that turnover brought changes. Now, our holiday plans are much different.

The drive to Grandma's place was always void of traffic and free from road hazards, unless you count those two railroad tracks that you had to pass right before you arrived at her house. They'd practically pitch you from the car.

You could smell the aromas of sage and celery even before you entered her back porch. That's where family and friends filtered through perpetually unlocked doors. Never mind knocking. Just come on in. Only strangers went to the formal front entry where the door was jammed.

Inside Grandma's house, the kitchen and dining areas were combined, making it all of two steps from the stove to the table. Since the cramped space wouldn't hold all of us, the youngsters sat on the back porch where they were grouped around wobbly card tables erected over bare concrete floors. Any cranberry stains or tea spills were sure to go unnoticed.

Tableware remained fully disposable, much like our manners. We'd gathered for fellowship, not airs or pretenses. The ambiance really didn't matter, though Grandma's house had its own.

After dinner, the men heeded some silent call only they could hear. Whatever its origin, it compelled them to collect in the den where they'd sit, transfixed, and scream at the Dallas Cowboys. The women went about cleaning the kitchen.

For entertainment, the children would search underneath the house for baby kittens and climb on farm equipment. But the ladies regrouped around the table once it had been restored. Keeping their voices low, they'd tell of events and stories they either couldn't or didn't want to talk about in front of their husbands. My admittance to this women's alliance was a rite of passage.

Now, two generations later, our family reunions have taken on a new form. Today's holiday meals are prepared in the suburbs, where you park at your own risk, and enter through the front door. The hostess displays her matching china on festive placemats. Often there are even coordinating cloth napkins. The centerpiece is a floral arrangement instead of Grandma's wisdoms.

The men are more participatory, herding kids and helping to clear the dishes from the table. However, they still group in the den and yell at the football players. And the children romp outdoors, though there are no farm animals to rustle up and no tractors to climb upon.

I suppose people must have their own mysterious migration processes because more than forty years have passed, yet the women continue to trickle back into the kitchen where they hover together and speak in hushed voices.

Men and Malls Don't Mix

ONLY ONE GENDER IS well-suited to shopping; men are too navigationally challenged to try to maneuver through a mall. That's a sexist statement, I know, but the truth isn't always politically correct. And I'm rarely serious, so I'll let you figure out which of these excuses applies.

Anyway, like I was trying to explain, men are simply disadvantaged. They've seldom had to exit a department store entrance and return through another for the sake of avoiding the Makeover Gal. And they've never had to calculate a course from shoes to sportswear that succeeds in bypassing cosmetics. Women, on the other hand, have been doing this ever since the birth of Sears.

Guys follow grids. Women look for landmarks—like Nordstrom and Dillard's. We automatically know how to find the opening to the mall's common areas by making a right at bras, a left at handbags, and another right at stupid-holiday-sweaters-you-would-only-wear-if-you-lived-at-the-North-Pole.

Men, however, just want to sail down unobstructed pathways at high speeds. They don't like to be sidetracked unless their distractions are:

a) female, b) sexually-provocative, c) persons offering free food samples, or d) all of the aforementioned.

One weekend in December, I made the tragic mistake of taking my spouse to a regional mall. Predictably, he balked before we'd even made it out of children's wear. I lead the way for him, fearlessly dodging strollers the size of farm equipment and hips that could only be photographed with a panorama lens.

My tailgater trailed behind me, muttering about the negative effects of consumerism and sensory overload. He was still complaining when his head whipsawed to the left. "Whoa, now," he exclaimed. "*That's something you might like for Christmas.*"

I turned and stared straight into a crotch.

There she was, a mannequin wearing thong underwear, a pair of black thigh-highs, and a Santa hat. "I'd rather have a body like that," I quipped.

Other than the Victoria's Secret display window, the only interests my mate has in shopping are those related to comforts. He can smell a Cinnabon from two corridors away and find a vibrating recliner even when it's been hidden in the Foley's china department.

But the worst part is when I start for the checkout counter. That's when he feigns a nervous collapse and crashes onto the first surface he sees. It might be a table display, or possibly the floor, or someone's unoccupied electric scooter. Mimicking a contortionist, he assumes a splayed position and the vacant stare of a lost preschooler. This elicits the immediate attention of compassionate store-goers and alert injury attorneys.

Usually, I drop my intended purchases, retrieve the shyster from his cast of sympathizers, and head for the house. There he makes a full recovery with only a brief treatment from a home-medical device called the television.

This idea occurred to me; if mall managers want to produce a significant spike in retail sales, they ought to eliminate the children's area in favor of a men's drop-off station. Instead of removing their shoes, like the little ones do, the anti-shoppers would be required to surrender their billfolds. While their wives blissfully troll for treasures, their mates would be free to partake of chair massages, televised sports, and unlimited servings of beer nuts chased with Gatorade.

These loitering loved ones could be monitored by retired grandmothers who long to have their grown sons return home. Working for a day or two at the men's drop-off station would give these enablers something to do with their time, while possibly curing their fantasies.

The men's station could be filled with vibrating chairs and other interactive products (which could be a boon for Brookstone). Guys are guaranteed to lose all sense of time when studying innovative technologies like sunglasses equipped with built-in camera phones.

I can only think of one hitch—these consumer displays would need to be arranged in a non-confusing and easy-to-navigate grid pattern.

Christmas Monopoly

FROM MORNING ROUTINES TO family customs, our lives are filled with rituals. I figured there was no time like the holidays to incorporate a new one into my repertoire. But trouble arrived when one of my four children suggested we add a Monopoly game to our holiday boredom prevention program.

My oldest son Ron and his wife Julie had driven into town to stay with us for a few days. Their visits, which typically last just about long enough to digest a meal, are always welcomed. However, this time they'd brought along with them the dog they endearingly called my "grand-puppy," a wiry-haired, hyperactive mixed breed with a vision problem. To this dog, everything must look like a tennis ball—because nothing is deemed unworthy of a good chase. So as you might imagine, our two cats were nonplussed about this houseguest.

After a food orgy that began at noon and continued well past the point of intestinal discomfort, I commenced pitching camp in front of the television. (I mean, let's face it; there's only so much eating you can do before every bathroom in the house is clogged.) It was time to yell, "Back away from the table, and put down your fork."

But just as I lifted the TV remote controller, Ron blurted, "Don't turn on the TV! Let's all *do* something together. You know, like family bonding."

First he says he's staying for two days, and now he says, "Don't turn on the television"? This can't be my child.

"I know," Ryan, my twelve-year-old, said. "Let's play MONOPOLY!"

Ron's face brightened. "Yeah. It'll be our new family tradition," he chimed.

Right then, I was glad I hadn't followed through on selling that game in my last garage sale.

As we gathered around the family dining table with Parker Brothers, the dog and one cat joined us. Each gave the other a suspicious eye, though thus far they'd been fairly tolerant.

About twenty minutes into the game, Ron said, "Hey, Mom, I'll give you these two blue ones for that railroad you're holding."

I didn't really need what he'd offered me, but I said, "Sure," anyway.

His eyes lit up as he snatched away my railroad card. "Suck-er-er-er-er!"

Okay. This is my child.

I'd forgotten how *long* a game of Monopoly can last. Ryan was the first to go bankrupt, so he moved into position to help me. Already, I'd given Ron his third of four railroads. What blunders were left?

If any family bonding was taking place, I hadn't yet observed it. More like it was every man, woman, child, and dog for himself.

My arms vibrated from all the table shaking that Ron's leg bouncing produced. His childhood tics had reemerged, the ones that had caused him to be sent home from school with report cards that said, "Refuses to sit still in class." That was back in the days before Ritalin.

Next, it was my husband's turn. He drew a Chance Card that condemned him to pay the last of his money to the remaining three players. "No-o-o!" he shouted, slamming his fist down onto the table.

The dog yelped. Then the cat, thinking she might be in jeopardy, attacked with a hiss and a few punches to the muzzle. Ryan fell out of his chair, laughing, and hurt his knee.

Julie, who was by now almost out of money, maintained a glum expression. So Ron looked lovingly into his wife's eyes and asked, "Would you like me to give you five hundred dollars for that railroad, Hon—just to keep you in the game?"

She gazed back at him and smiled. "Would ya?"

"Of course. What are husbands for?" he gushed. Then he whisked the card from her hand and hollered, "All R–R–I–I–I–IGHT!"

No one was surprised when eventually Ron won the game, and he was the only one who went to bed happy that night. My husband felt his position as "head-of-household" had been usurped. Julie had been deceived by her own spouse. The other children had been once again outdone by their older brother. And thanks to this entire ruckus, the dog and cat now had more trust issues than ever before.

That evening, I fell asleep and dreamed about traipsing cross-county to view exterior illumination like most normal families do.

This year, we'll need to establish a new holiday ritual—because the most I got out of that Monopoly game was the two bucks it brought during last summer's garage sale.

Time for Trouble

WATCHES ARE FREQUENT SELECTIONS among gift givers. But I'm watch phobic. No timepiece for this gal. No-sir-ee.

Like most of my irrational behaviors, this lingering fear stems from early painful experiences. For me, a watch is a ticking messenger of doom.

My abhorrence of timekeepers can be traced back to my first love. Now, this wasn't a puppy love. It was more like the full-grown St. Bernard variety, a young and innocent relationship that lead me to the worst kind of heartbreak a girl can suffer and still survive. I not only wanted to be part of this guy's present, but also his past and future.

Everything about my newfound heartthrob was terminally interesting to me, right down to his rugged, blue-dial watch. He was happy to share with me the history of his accessory's origin, too. This masculine fashion statement, it turned out, had been given to him by *his* first love, a Christmas gift received during his senior year in high school. He explained how the girl who lived next door to his family's home had been his childhood sweetheart. They'd grown up together, experienced early intimacy with each other, yadda, yadda, yadda. Definitely more than I wanted to know about his stupid watch.

Not long after that, I stopped asking him for the time.

Over the Christmas holidays that year, my boyfriend returned to his hometown to visit his parents, the people who lived next door to Ms. Timex (not her real name). It simply wouldn't have been appropriate for me to come along, I was told. So on Christmas Eve, I sat home alone and thought a lot about watches.

This old girlfriend of his had been quite cunning. She'd probably bought that gift so my fellow would have to think of her every time he looked at it. She must have known her beau would soon be departing for college and that they'd inevitably be separated. The timepiece, she may have felt, would be more durable than his long-term memory. And darn it, she'd been right.

My guy returned to me on New Year's Eve, wearing a new cologne scent and a narcotic smile. He laughed about seeing his old heartthrob and the awkwardness of their brief visit. The flame was certainly gone, but he appeared to be smoldering.

More than once the thought had crossed my mind to buy him a new watch. However, that would have made my jealousy a bit too obvious. Besides, I told myself, I was still in the picture. He didn't need a reminder of me.

Months passed, and one day I noticed that his calls had become infrequent. Soon he began arriving late for our dates. It was September, and fall was upon us. I could feel it.

On my birthday, he took me out for a nice dinner, and after the meal he presented me with an exquisitely wrapped, rectangular package. Inside I found a lady's watch.

"It's already set," he assured me.

And it certainly was. But without even looking, I knew the time.

Diana Estill

Diana Estill has been a journalist and humor columnist for ten years. Her work has appeared online, in magazines, and in major newspapers, including *The Washington Post, The Miami Herald,* and *The Dallas Morning News.* She was a finalist in the August 2005 *America's Funniest Humor* Contest.

Diana lives with her husband in North Texas, where she claims authorities will issue most anyone a valid driver's license.